Reputation Strategy and Analytics in a Hyper-Connected World

Reputation Strategy and Analytics in a Hyper-Connected World

Chris Foster

WILEY

Published by John Wiley & Sons, Inc., Hoboken, New Jersey.
Published simultaneously in Canada.

For general information on our other products and services or for technical support, please contact our Customer Care Department within the United States at (800) 762-2974, outside the United States at (317) 572-3993, or fax (317) 572-4002.

Wiley publishes in a variety of print and electronic formats and by print-on-demand. Some material included with standard print versions of this book may not be included in e-books or in print-on-demand. If this book refers to media such as a CD or DVD that is not included in the version you purchased, you may download this material at http://booksupport.wiley.com. For more information about Wiley products, visit www.wiley.com.

Library of Congress Cataloging-in-Publication Data:

Title: Reputation strategy and analytics in a hyper-connected world / Chris Foster.
Description: Hoboken: Wiley, 2016.
Identifiers: LCCN 2016014398 | ISBN 978-1-119-05249-4 (cloth) | ISBN 978-1-119-21270-6 (ePDF) | ISBN 978-1-119-21271-3 (ePUB)
Subjects: LCSH: Corporate image. | Communication in management. | BISAC: BUSINESS & ECONOMICS / Business Communication / General.
Classification: LCC HD59.2 .F67 2016 | DDC 659.2--dc23 LC record available at https://lccn.loc.gov/2016014398

Printed in the United States of America
10 9 8 7 6 5 4 3 2 1

Contents

Acknowledgments

T he contents of this book are based primarily on my hands-on experiences in the corporate communications field over the past two decades. The book also represents a process of discovery, in which I sought the opinions and wisdom of numerous experts. In that respect, the book is a trove of collected knowledge and insight, enriched by persistent research and interviews with many expert sources, including Erin Byrne, Lauren Coleman, Yasmin Crowther, Patrick "Pat" Ford, Martis "Marty" Davis, Bronwyn Kunhardt, Eric McNulty, and Ame Wadler, who generously shared their stories and insight with me. I thank them sincerely for their time, their energy, their intelligence, and their kindness.

This book would not have been possible without the effort, attention, and steady guidance of Jeanine Moss, the founder and president of Turning Point Solutions. Jeanine is truly one of the best strategic communications advisors in the field, and I greatly value her friendship.

I owe a special debt of gratitude to Mike Barlow, who served as editorial director for this book. His advice and expertise were invaluable. Thank you, Mike!

I also extend my sincere thanks to Sheck Cho and Vincent Nordhaus, my editors at John Wiley & Sons, who had faith in the value of the project and were patient when I missed my deadlines.

Most of all, I want to thank my wife, Jan, and our son, Nicholas, for their love, support, and willingness to take this journey with me—thank you!

Introduction

We live in a world of increasing transparency and high velocity communications. Information not only travels faster, it travels farther and is available everywhere. The rapid convergence of cloud, social, and mobile technologies has created a new generation of empowered and information hungry customers.

In today's interconnected consumer economy, the notion that a company's reputation can be "managed" as a simple commodity or one-dimensional artifact is dangerously outdated. Every morsel of information—no matter how trivial or seemingly innocuous—has the potential to go viral in a heartbeat. Reputations that took decades to build can be destroyed in mere moments.

Brand Does Not Equal Reputation

Great companies discern the critical difference between brand and reputation. Let's take a moment to examine this difference, because it is vitally important. As customers, our impression of a brand is usually formed by our direct experiences with a company's products or services.

A company's reputation, however, is formed by a collective belief system about quality or character. These beliefs are typically formed from hearing or reading the opinions of other people—friends, experts, and even total strangers—which today are relayed across an ever-widening array of media platforms and channels.

A good reputation:

- **Creates trust** in an organization's products or services
- **Provides access** to policy and decision makers
- **Attracts and retains** the best employees
- **Drives credibility** with outside partners
- Serves as a **critical success factor** for investors

Indeed, the difference between brand and reputation is huge, and not yet fully appreciated. The management of a brand is a multidimensional function ranging from communications to product marketing. It involves complex and interrelated programs with often fuzzy mechanisms for measuring results or gleaning data that would improve future efforts. The reputation of a brand, on the other hand, is affected by additional factors that are independent of marketing-oriented brand management activities. Market conditions, CEO performance, and employee churn are all examples of variables that affect corporate reputation.

With that in mind, it's fair to say that the reputation of a brand reflects a broad and fluid set of perceptions, beliefs, and expectations held by all of an organization's stakeholders. It is the sum of their opinions, based largely on what they see, read, hear, and experience.

Reputation Strategy: The Proof of a Successful Brand Management Program

Until fairly recently, the downside risk of confusing brand and reputation, or not understanding how the mechanics of brand management and Reputation Strategy differ, was relatively minor. However, the Internet, broadband networks, and handheld mobile devices have changed all of that. Now, the risks are higher and the downsides are considerably steeper.

Before the era of 24/7 media, reputational damage could be managed and mitigated by skillful public relations teams or corporate communications executives. In the rapidly evolving global information landscape, however, stakeholders have greater access to information and can easily uncover actions, behaviors, decisions, or values that are incongruous with communications of the organization. Today, news travels faster and farther than ever before and communications professionals need the support of additional capabilities and tools to be effective.

The complexity of managing this "always on" environment can cause one to lose perspective, focusing on the deluge of big data while losing sight of the larger story that the data tells. But Reputation Strategy becomes the tangible proof of how well the brand is doing and the beacon lighting the way by detecting the big ideas in the data details.

A Delicate Balance of Multiple Inputs

Reputation is an outcome of organizational behavior, values, decisions, and actions. Unlike traditional tangible assets, it is both multidimensional and fluid. Although intangible, reputation management can be integrated into business planning and operationally embedded into organizational approaches across business units and geographies to positively affect a company's valuation, sales, employee morale, performance, partnerships, and a host of other critical areas.

Reputation can be leveraged for strategic advantage through insights gained from the scientific application of real-time big data analytics and multidisciplinary approaches.

Building reputation is not an entirely new idea. But the application of scientific methods incorporating advanced analytics brings new capabilities for prediction and optimization, which reveal new opportunities and genuine advantages.

More than just a technique for managing reputation, Reputation Strategy is derived from a carefully orchestrated set of scientific processes that create and sustain competitive advantage in a turbulent world.

Reputation is not monolithic. It is assembled from thousands of data points across stakeholder groups and markets. Thus, reputation is complex and cannot be simplified to a single score or index. A forward-thinking organization will take deliberate steps to monitor and analyze data that might affect its reputation. More important, it will take proactive steps to build its reputation on a solid foundation, one brick at a time.

I believe that data is the key to successful Reputation Strategy at virtually every level. Our ability to ingest and integrate multiple data sets from a wide variety of sources is changing the practice of communications. Organizations that are using data and data science to support communications in these ways will be more competitive and the insights generated will inform a more effective strategy.

New Tools for Extracting Value from Streams of Data

The rise of big data and data science has given us new tools and techniques for extracting value from information, revealing hidden patterns, and uncovering fresh insights. New database technologies and advanced analytics solutions enable us to blend knowledge and expertise from multiple industries and markets, improving business outcomes and driving faster cycles of innovation in hyper-competitive markets.

In today's communications environment, big data acts like an accelerant. Issues that took years or months to unfold now spin wildly out of control in hours or minutes. Clipping newspaper articles, holding focus groups, commissioning surveys, hiring mystery shoppers, or trying to embargo stories—those kinds of tactics worked fine in an age when there were only three major television networks and essentially one national telephone company.

Events happen much more quickly now; news travels much faster. As a result, opinions are formed more quickly, and reputations can be damaged or destroyed within days or hours.

Given the dynamics of today's interconnected global culture, Reputation Strategy requires a blend of business intelligence, big data analytics, predictive modeling, and forecasting capabilities. Traditional reputation management tools and approaches are often inadequate for dealing with modern day challenges.

Reputation Strategy is a combination of business acumen and scientific expertise. It should be used as an ongoing strategy to propel and protect business objectives, but it cannot be conjured up or improvised at the last moment or in the face of a crisis. It must be staffed and fully functioning before the crisis. Waiting until the emergency arises virtually guarantees a bad outcome.

Reputation Exists in a Complex Communications Ecosystem

Reputation cannot be judged, described, or distinguished at a glance. Multiple streams of data from multiple sources must be collected, integrated, analyzed, evaluated, and harvested for insight that can be used to develop meaningful responses to changes or shifts in reputation. Since reputation is built from an aggregate of many components, different approaches are required for different companies and different markets.

Reputation Strategy is composed of multiple action steps and processes based on environmental factors as well as factors within an organization's sphere of influence (Figure I.1). Through the application of Reputation Strategy, scalable, repeatable, reliable, and predictable actions can be taken.

Figure I.1 Stakeholder Perceptions and Expectations

Every organization has a unique set of attributes that can be classified into those that could affect existing value or those that could generate new value. This allows organizations to address risks and issues as well as proactively identify and address opportunities.

For example, reputation can be leveraged to create business advantages in supply chain relationships, executive talent recruiting, sales, sourcing, finance, and other functional areas of the modern enterprise.

In a recent engagement with a global firm, we integrated multiple types of data into a single model, making it possible for our client to recognize how each issue contributed to its reputation and how those issues affected the firm's reputation across its ecosystem of stakeholders.

Based on our analysis, we identified activities that should be created, sustained, or eliminated to better support reputation goals. With a comprehensive understanding of the factors or "drivers" underlying the company's reputation, we helped them devise a workable strategy for influencing it.

Prediction Is Key to Better Outcomes

Big data and real-time analytics create essential capabilities for modeling, comparing, and predicting outcomes of reputational issues. I recently led an engagement in which an interdisciplinary team of experts generated real-time predictive indicators of reputational impact for a client and tested multiple scenarios for how to address a situation based on our Reputation Analytics Framework (Figure I.2). We also created a reporting framework that helped our client understand their reputation globally and develop strategies for protecting and enhancing their reputation over time.

Over the course of the engagement, we performed research, data integration, data/driver analysis (predictive and descriptive), strategy development, and change management analysis. The results of our work provided visibility into resource allocation and critical insights that informed future situations.

We took the following action steps:

- Developed an early warning system to let our client know which stakeholders in what markets would be affected by specific aspects of their reputation.

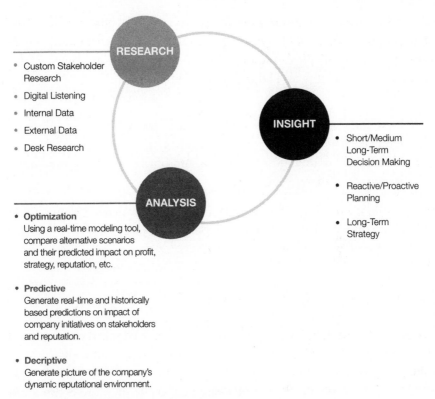

Figure I.2   Reputation Analytics Framework

- Customized and delivered our Reputation Intelligence Model to:
  - Integrate the wide range of data streams we identified so that our client could understand stakeholder relationships and their causes.
  - Align program initiatives with corporate strategic objectives to indicate impact and assist with strategic planning and efficacy analysis.

The engagement reinforced my belief that successful implementation of data analytics involves various departments and functional areas of the modern enterprise working in close collaboration. It includes departments like IT, communications, operations, human resources; functions like data science and business strategy; and subject matter experts.

The key word is *collaboration*. Experience shows that the total is always more than the sum of its parts.

Addressing reputational challenges successfully requires:

- Building a framework to enable reputation to be used as a strategic advantage with customers, governments, partners, and employees.
- Monitoring, evaluating, analyzing, and responding appropriately in real time.
- Predicting where and how communications will have an effect on reputation (for example, crisis life cycle, regression analysis).
- Learning how to allocate resources appropriately to gain maximum Reputation Strategy advantage.

While it is possible to outsource certain components of Reputation Strategy, companies should also consider developing their own internal expertise and experience.

Reputation Is Not a Momentary Phenomenon

Reputation building is a long-term strategic endeavor. It is an integrated set of ongoing processes, not an individual program, campaign, or one-shot initiative.

Moreover, reputation is not a singular event or state. Reputation has multiple states and forms. It changes over time—sometimes slowly, sometimes with breathtaking speed. Building a reputation that is strong, resilient, and not fragile requires top down leadership, executive sponsorship, and buy-in at all levels of the enterprise. It requires written policies, training, incentives, and discipline. The concept of *reputation as a strategy* must be woven into the culture of the organization.

In great, progressive companies, reputation is an integral part of the cultural DNA. It isn't an afterthought; it's top of mind.

Don't Try This at Home

Because Reputation Strategy is core to a company's operations, with complex requirements for data, processes, and people, this transformation should not be thought of as a "do it yourself" or "back of the envelope" affair. Smart organizations will set aside the time and devote the resources necessary for creating and sustaining practical reputation strategies.

Reputation Strategy is a set of scientific multidisciplinary processes that must be integrated into business planning and embedded into operations across business units and geographies, with the proper executive sponsorship. Ultimately, accountability sits at the highest level of the organization. The CEO and the board must drive awareness of the strategy and keep employees at all levels engaged.

Net Takeaway

In a transparent world, reputation is a strategic asset and core competency requiring a blend of communications analytics, data science, and multidisciplinary expertise. It should be treated as a competitive business advantage.

Reputation Strategy provides tangible value to organizations through:

- Creating trust in the organization's products and services
- Providing access to policy and decision makers
- Attracting and retaining the best employees
- Driving credibility with outside partners
- Serving as a critical success factor for investors

Reputation must be protected and enhanced through authentic organizational values, decisions, behaviors, and actions. It requires a clear and evidence-based Reputation Strategy, based on a carefully orchestrated portfolio of analytics that illuminates consumer attitudes and creates predictive models that anticipate consumer behavior.

Reputation Strategy and Analytics in a Hyper-Connected World

Chapter One

Welcome to the Networked Ecosystem

Executive Summary: In a digital networked ecosystem with no clear time or physical boundaries, traditional strategies and tactics deployed by communication professionals will not work, and might even be harmful. Newer and more agile methods based on careful data analysis and scientific reasoning are required.

These days, it seems as though every executive feels obligated to talk about the critical need for collecting data, managing data, analyzing data, storing data, and harvesting insights from data. All of those activities are important, but what's even more important is creating a corporate culture in which data is respected, valued, and understood. From my perspective, the primary barrier to extracting value from data is culture, not technology.

1

The processes of data science are inherently collaborative and cross-disciplinary, which essentially means you cannot do data science in a vacuum. It cannot be relegated to the basement or to a back room. It's a team sport. There are plenty of moving parts that require careful orchestration and dedicated leadership.

Too often I see data siloed in specialized groups or I hear people talking about using data to generate insights. Your organization can have all the insights in the world, but they will not help unless you have a culture that knows how to transform those insights into ideas and effective decisions.

In the twenty-first-century economy, data is the fuel we use to make better decisions. It's the raw material from which we manufacture success. We have to use that data and then take action.

Changing the Culture

Saying that an organization is "data driven" doesn't mean it's being run by computers. It means that key decisions are informed and influenced by evidence, which is derived from data. Not every decision needs to be made by human beings—an increasing number of decisions can be delegated to software applications and other forms of automation. For example, you don't need a human to decide whether to turn on the air conditioning in the summer. That kind of decision can and should be automated.

For the most part, we're fine with delegating straightforward decisions to machines. But now there's a widening area in which we're not so sure how much decision-making power we really want to share with our software applications. For example, farmers used to decide when to water their crops. Now, exquisitely complex systems of machinery, software, mobile devices, and sensors—including cameras mounted on airborne drones and orbiting satellites—decide when it's necessary to turn on the spigot.

The real question facing us is whether we want to use our increasingly sophisticated decision-making technology not just to grow better grapes and keep our shopping malls cool in the summer, but to improve the performance of our companies and organizations.

The question that executives should be asking is not about technology. For the most part, the technology you need to make better decisions is already available. The question executives need to ask is this: How do we transform our organizations into data-driven cultures?

The Digital Revolution Has Rewritten the Rules

It's not exactly fresh news that digital information technologies have changed everything, but it's worth repeating: Digital information technologies have changed everything.

On many levels, we all understand that we're living through a revolution, but the reality has not fully set in. In the communications industry, for example, most of us pay lip service to "new media," but few of us are genuinely comfortable operating within the digital environment, which now surrounds and envelops us so completely.

Some of my best friends still pine for "the good old days" when most of our business was done at lunches or over the phone. I also experience a twinge of nostalgia and fondness for the past. It's only natural. In the past, everything was easier, simpler, and slower. Or at least, it seems that way.

What we had then, that we don't have now, is a routine. There is no well-worn path or standard operating procedure—yet. For decades, we relied on a comparatively narrow set of reflexive responses to whatever challenges came our way. Table 1.1 is a gross simplification, but it will remind you of how we typically dealt with problems before everyone had a computer, a smartphone, and a Facebook account.

Table 1.1 Typical Responses of Functional Silos Operating within Traditional Organizations

Communications Function	Standard Response
Public relations	*Write a press release*
Media relations	*Call a reporter*
Corporate communications	*Send a company-wide memo*
Marketing communications	*Write a brochure*
Advertising	*Place ads in traditional media (print, radio, TV, billboard)*

Collaborating, Crowdsourcing, and Co-Creating

Modern digital technologies don't merely help us manage larger amounts of information more quickly—they enable us to interact with the information we handle. We are no longer passive customers of information—we sample it, we modify it, and we share the results of our improvised tinkering across the social networks that we help to create. Today, everyone is a publisher.

In the past, developing and distributing content required significant upfront investments of capital. You needed lots of money to buy printing presses and television transmitters. And you needed even more money to hire people with the skills, talent, and experience necessary to create content that you could distribute profitably to a large audience. Publishing and broadcasting companies were run like factories—products were manufactured from component materials and then distributed through various channels to customers.

Digital information technologies have liberated content creation from that industrial model. Some would argue that content creation has been democratized. To some extent, that is true. But I think it would be more accurate to say that content is increasingly created through collaboration and crowdsourcing. At any given hour of any given day, we are interacting with content and co-creating new content.

Why is that relevant to all of us in the communications industry? It's relevant because it means we need a new playbook. The rules have changed. The game has changed. We need to change.

Constant Change Is the New Normal: Welcome to the "Always On" Era

In hindsight, it seems as though we had been living in a placid universe when events unfolded with predictable linearity. Suddenly, and without warning, we find ourselves thrust into a turbulent universe in which events occur in unpredictable patterns at lightning speed.

In this new universe, no one gets to dictate the terms of engagement. Dynamism is the new reality. Constant change is the new normal. In a universe in which every customer is "always on," instantly able to find the lowest price, the best deal, and the fastest mode of delivery, no brand can afford to be "sort of on" and count on customer loyalty for very long.

The old playbook assumed that brands would talk and customers would listen. The new playbook makes no such assumption. The new playbook is based on our awareness—and acceptance—of an empowered public, armed with all the tools and skills of the digital age. The empowered public doesn't sit still, hates being categorized, and is always looking out for the next new wave. Engaging with them requires a new mindset, a different set of skills, and a deep understanding of their inherent dynamism. In the new universe, dynamic engagement drives communication strategy and generates real business outcomes.

Dynamic Engagement versus Traditional Communication

Unlike traditional approaches to communication, dynamic engagement assumes that tactics must be adapted to the situation. Context is everything. Just because Plan A worked for Client B last year doesn't guarantee that it will magically work for Client C this year. Data can point the way toward applying previously successful solutions, adapting them to a new situation, or finding an altogether new solution.

Dynamic engagement is like cooking—people get bored when you serve the same meal, and they can always tell when you don't use fresh ingredients.

Traditional strategies were a blend of art and science, with the emphasis strongly on art. There was a general belief in the power of instinct—"gut feelings"—over the power of process. In this book, we will argue in favor of a more balanced and carefully reasoned approach.

Our argument is based on the simple truth that in today's digitally connected hyper-reactive global culture, events unfold so rapidly that relying primarily on our gut feelings to solve complex problems would be the height of arrogance.

And since we all know that pride comes before a fall, let's agree to ditch the arrogance and accept the reality that we can no longer control the message. The genie is out of the bottle, the ship has sailed, and the die is cast.

In F. Scott Fitzgerald's novel *The Great Gatsby,* Nick Carraway warns Jay Gatsby, "You can't repeat the past," and yet sometimes it seems as though many people in our industry are trying to do exactly that—repeat the past. Why? I think that the need to be "always on" in today's media world leads many of us to want to react immediately, and the simplest way to do that is to repeat what has worked for us in the past. It also offers the comfort of a solution that can be easily defended, because it was used before.

Dynamic engagement does not ask us to react reflexively, but rather to respond in near real time, thoughtfully applying the data we have available. It also asks us to be comfortable with the idea that we may be wrong, and many of us are not comfortable with that idea, especially in stressful circumstances. We prefer a thoughtful but possibly imperfect response over a thoughtless repetition of the past.

Applying the ER Model to PR

Dynamic engagement doesn't aim for perfection—it aims for results. When you're wheeled into a hospital emergency room, you don't need TV's Sanjay Gupta. You need effective treatment that's fast, appropriate, and based on science.

From my perspective, dynamic engagement is similar to the kind of medicine practiced in a modern emergency room. It's highly collaborative—you need a team of well-trained specialists, working together, to achieve a common goal.

The traditional communication team was composed mostly of liberal arts majors. There's nothing wrong with that—I majored in philosophy at college, and nothing is more liberal-artsy than philosophy! But my graduate degree is in applied behavioral counseling, and the scientific training I acquired in graduate school has proven immensely helpful over the course of my career.

A dynamic engagement team would include some liberal arts majors. It might also include an economist, a data analyst, a social scientist, a behavioral psychologist, an app developer, a webmaster, a media relations expert, and someone with hands-on knowledge of the specific business or industry we're trying to help.

The team would be diverse, since it would be expected to create a diverse set of effective solutions. Diversity isn't merely a nice thing to have—when you're dealing with diverse markets, you need to assemble a team of people with diverse skills and experiences. You need doers, not talkers—people who can size up a situation, come up with a solution on the fly, and get to work fast.

It's a complex world, and you need a team that can handle complexity. I can state categorically that I could never have accomplished any of my professional goals without the support of great people and great teamwork.

Consider the Communication Ecosystem

Dynamic engagement does not take place in a vacuum. It takes place within a noisy ecosystem of interrelated parties and platforms.

Think of it as an expanding multinode network. Everything is connected, and some connections are more critical than others. Moreover, the importance and value of the connections within the network are continuously changing. You never step into the same river twice.[1]

Because the ecosystem is continuously changing, a set of tactics that worked just fine yesterday might not work at all today. In a world of dynamic engagement, you need quick reflexes. You have to be fast, flexible, agile, and comfortable with continuous change. There is no status quo.

If you hate being stuck in a rut, that should come as good news. Dynamic engagement abhors a rut—you never have enough time to dig yourself into one!

There's nothing more comforting than the illusion that a solution you invented last year will help you solve a problem this year. But clinging to an illusion isn't going to help you or your client.

Let me share a story that illustrates why it's absolutely essential to understand the ecosystem. I've modified a few of the minor details to avoid embarrassing anyone. A client in the medical device industry had experienced some quality issues with one of its products, and a local newspaper had printed a negative article about the company on its front page. A senior executive called my team in a panic. "Everyone," they told us, "is saying bad things about the company." The client wanted us to prepare an "open letter" apology that would run as a full-page advertisement in several major newspapers.

In the past, running a full-page apology in a handful of large newspapers might have been part of a larger solution to help the company restore its damaged reputation.

But instead of rushing headlong into action—which would have made our team look exceedingly brave and heroic—we decided to slow down the pace and take a good, hard look at the ecosystem in which the problem was unfolding.

It turned out that "everyone" wasn't saying bad things about the client. In fact, the vast majority of people weren't even aware of the problem. Yes, there had been some newspaper articles. But they hadn't ignited a firestorm of controversy.

A thorough examination revealed that most of the trash talk was confined to a couple of Internet chat rooms used primarily by a handful of analysts who covered the medical devices industry. The problem was real, but it didn't rise to the level of requiring full-page apologies in the *New York Times,* the *Wall Street Journal,* and *USA Today.*

Our analysis of the problem, which took the ecosystem into account, led us to devise a simpler and less dramatic solution. Buying full-page ads in national newspapers would have been like pouring gasoline onto a smoldering fire. In addition to attracting more attention, it would have been very expensive. Our solution was effective and significantly less costly.

Part of our success in this particular instance was due to preparation. We had foreseen earlier that the ability to examine multiple parts of the ecosystem might be important, and so we had begun to develop contextual "listening" capabilities required to understand how conversations arise, evolve, and often migrate across platforms. In other words, we didn't just say, "Hey, let's check the ecosystem before buying those full-page ads." We had been practicing and honing our skills long before the client came to us with its problem.

Here's another example, also from the health care industry. Our client was a large company that made a variety of medications for people with cardiovascular disease. As most of us will agree, those types of medications—which include drugs to reduce hypertension, lower cholesterol levels, and control diabetes—can be real lifesavers. They also help people stay out the hospital, and greatly reduce the chances of having a stroke or heart attack.

The company was trying to promote awareness of its medications within the African-American community, which suffers a disproportionately large share of cardiovascular ailments. The company had made some modest efforts, but they hadn't been particularly effective. They asked us to figure out a better way of reaching out to the African-American market.

We were aware that churches and other faith-based organizations often play large roles in African-American communities. We knew African-American communities might distrust or ignore information from sources that were overtly connected to the existing establishment power structures.

Based on our understanding of the ecosystem, we launched a faith-based health information initiative designed specifically to serve African-American markets. We integrated health with spirituality, leveraging the inherent power of local churches and ministries to reach their congregants and convey a positive message.

The initiative was a huge success. Through a partnership with Sharon Allison-Ottey, MD, who serves as executive director and director of health and community initiatives of the COSHAR Foundation, we eventually created a network of faith-based organizations that actively promoted the value and benefits of health information. We also discovered that for the African-American audience, radio was a highly effective medium for sharing health information—especially during drive time on Sunday mornings, when many families were heading to church.

If we had taken the easy path and followed the established road map for launching a campaign to build awareness, we would have connected with only a tiny slice of the potential audience. Instead, we blazed our own trail, customizing our programs to fit the needs of the real-world ecosystem of our audience.

Early in my career, I was taught to create psychological profiles of stakeholders within a market or demographic segment we wanted to reach. Those profiles were used to guide our messaging and campaigns. Today, I'm not a big fan of that approach. As a practical matter, without data to inform the bigger ecosystem within which that cohort or "stakeholder" group operates in our engagements, no one is really sure what it means. Customer profiling or "stakeholders" exist as entities within larger ecosystems, as the poet John Donne wrote a long time ago:

No man is an island,
Entire of itself,
Every man is a piece of the continent,
A part of the main.

Those words were true when Donne wrote them in 1623, and they remain true today.

Follow the Conversation—Wherever It Goes

Until very recently, the impact of conversation was severely constrained by distance. Even if you were shouting, your voice would carry only a couple of hundred yards. The invention of writing, followed by subsequent innovations such as the printing press and movable type, made it possible for conversations to spread beyond village boundaries.

In the nineteenth century, electricity made it possible to transmit conversations across long distance through wires. The invention of radio removed the restraints imposed by the need for wires, and enabled conversations to move freely across vast stretches of land and ocean.

In the twentieth century, radio and television brought conversations to every corner of the Earth, creating what communication theorist Marshall McLuhan described as a new "global village" in which the human experience was profoundly transformed by electronic technology. Toward the end of the twentieth century and in the early years of the twenty-first century, the Internet and the World Wide Web emerged as robust platforms facilitating interactive communications among billions of people. In the past several years, mobile has expanded the reach of the web to even more people, including people in parts of the world with little or no direct access to the Internet. Mobile is rapidly developing its own unique ecosystem for enabling conversations.

Moreover, the convergence of various technologies has created a dense tangle of interlocking sub-ecosystems. Conversations no longer begin and end in one place. They move all over—increasingly, they can move across the planet, in minutes.

Today, it's not unusual for a story—or a rumor—to begin on an obscure website and get picked up by the online edition of a newspaper or magazine. From there, it gets tweeted and shared on Facebook. People see it on their smartphones, and they text snippets of it to their friends. Pretty soon, it's on Reddit. Then it gets noticed by the search engines: Google, Yahoo!, Baidu, and Bing. Someone might post a quick video on YouTube or a six-second looping video clip on Vine. Some of the digerati will blog about the story, posting on various platforms, such as WordPress, Blogger, Typepad, and Tumblr.

A story that started as a whisper can now be seen within hours or even minutes by billions of people. If the story persists, it might even make it onto Wikipedia. Sadly, the story doesn't even have to be true or accurate to spread like a virus. It just has to be interesting enough for people to want to share it with their friends. Welcome to the new communication ecosystem. No one is in charge. Many people consider that a good thing. Many people don't.

No matter where you stand on the relative merits of the new communication ecosystem, you need to understand how it works. It's like riding the subway in New York City. You don't have to love it, but it sure helps to know the difference between the A-train and the 1-train on a rainy day when you can't get an Uber or Lyft and your only hope of getting to your meeting on time is taking the subway.

For example, our team here at Burson-Marsteller knows how to track conversations as they move from one platform to another. We know the techniques for measuring the real-world impact of online conversations, and we can tell whether those conversations are merely irritating or doing serious damage to your brand.

It's not just stories and rumors that are flying in every direction. Your audience is in motion, too. They're constantly shifting networks, platforms, and devices. Think about it for a moment: You start the day by checking the messages on your phone. On the train to work, you watch a video on your tablet. At the office, you boot up your laptop and start working on a slide presentation for an upcoming meeting with a new client. In between, you're checking Twitter, Facebook, and Instagram.

Your customers do the same thing. Tracking them as they flit like butterflies across the digital universe isn't easy, but the alternative—being clueless about what they are doing—is worse.

Time Is Not on Our Side

When I was growing up, most daily newspapers had two editions—an "early" edition for commuters and a "late" edition for home delivery. Big city newspapers had several editions, including a "bulldog" edition that hit the streets the night before the regular editions were published. If some incredibly newsworthy event occurred, a newspaper might publish an "extra"—or simply make its readers wait until the next morning to find out what happened.

Publishing multiple editions of a daily newspaper was a complex task that required special skills, deep knowledge of the community, and the ability to coordinate and choreograph a diverse set of finite resources within a fairly tight frame of time.

Despite its complexity, that task seems like child's play compared to what editors, publishers, and broadcasters face today. The traditional "news cycle" has vanished. In the past, a talented public relations team could manage the flow and slant of news quite effectively by simply staying a few hours ahead of a newspaper's copy deadlines. In the modern media environment, there are simply too many outlets to keep track of—and there are no firm deadlines.

Newspaper copy deadlines were set to make sure the printing presses ran on time. The presses had to run on time so the trucks that carried the bundles of printed newspapers would leave the loading dock in time to deliver the bundles to the hundreds of shops and stores that sold the newspapers. For a newspaper, every day was like D-Day—a huge logistical challenge with multiple points of potential failure.

Modern news organizations don't have to worry so much about making sure the presses run on time—because in many cases, there aren't any presses. Sure, there are still newspapers that print ink-on-paper editions, but most of today's news is consumed on PCs, laptops, tablets, and smartphones.

Even TV news is beginning to seem quaint and old-fashioned. Unless you're stuck in an airport or working out at the gym, how often do you spend more than a couple of minutes watching "the news" on a television set?

The media landscape is fragmented, our attention spans are limited, and we're constantly racing from one place to another to attend a meeting, catch a bus, pick up the kids, watch a game, or meet for drinks after work. We're living longer, and yet it seems like we have less time.

That isn't just a complaint—it's a stark reality that has totally and permanently transformed the communications industry.

Let's face it: Time is no longer on our side. Customers are living the always-on dream, able to personalize and customize their real-time data, connectivity, and content. In effect, the customer has become a webmaster of real-time data, adeptly managing news streams, social updates, and unified inboxes.

Companies, by contrast, lag way behind in realizing the always-on dream. This is largely because companies still struggle to master the data that can propel actionable, practical business-building programs. In the past, we could rely on our understanding of how the media worked—and our knowledge of media deadlines—to control or influence the flow of news.

We no longer can count on that advantage. Back in "the good old days," it was common practice to release bad news after 5 P.M. on Friday because it meant the story wouldn't appear in the newspaper until Saturday, when fewer readers picked up the newspaper. With careful timing and good luck, a skillful PR team could practically bury a story—or at least mitigate its impact.

In today's media ecosystem, the news cycle is continuous and "always on." Stories never completely disappear; they just move lower on your news feed. There's a memorable bit in the movie *Chef* in which Jon Favreau's character, an emotionally overwrought chef, tweets a pithy insult to a famous food critic who has just panned his menu. When the tweet goes viral, the chef is astonished to discover that he cannot simply have the offending tweet expunged from the Internet. He remains apoplectic, even when a sympathetic PR adviser reminds him that in a few days, no one will remember what he tweeted.

I'm not going to spoil the plot by revealing more. Suffice it to say that the harsh lesson in Twitter etiquette proves handy later on. I recommend *Chef* to anyone in the communications industry, especially if you also like movies about food.

Go with the Data? Not Always . . .

Remember that data is not reality—it's just a useful way of looking at reality. Even the best data is usually just a slice or a fragment of a much larger picture. And you can't always be sure you're looking at the most relevant data, or that the data you're looking at is the data that your client really cares about.

Here's an example to illustrate this point. The client was a hospital, and several of its top executives had called me in to discuss ways for improving the hospital's reputation ranking. We talked for a while, and it soon became apparent that the reason they were worried was because the hospital's CEO was very focused on rankings and they wanted to keep the CEO happy.

Following my own "Stop, look, and listen" advice, I suggested we all take a deep breath and look at the reputation ranking as part of the ecosystem. After all, I reminded them, the ranking isn't some kind of freestanding entity with magical power that points to either certain doom or certain success. It's merely an indicator.

Moreover, it's not even one of the primary indicators used by people when they're choosing a hospital. A hospital's ranking is one of two dozen or more criteria that factor into someone's decision to choose one hospital over another. When you really think about it, is a hospital's ranking the first piece of information you think about, or is it your doctor's, friend's, or family's recommendation?

The moral here is that not all data is created equal. Some data is more important than other data, and you can't allow yourself or your client to get overly focused on data that doesn't strongly affect the client's reputation or performance in a particular market.

I'm not recommending that you ignore data that isn't immediately relevant. But you have to keep a close watch on your audience to know which data is truly relevant and which data is merely distracting you from solving the real problem.

Four Common Mistakes

It's hard to imagine a time of greater change for the communications industry. We're plunging forward rapidly into a universe in which the old rules don't apply. We're collectively co-creating the new playbook as we go. We're adopting new tools, technologies, and techniques to deal with an ecosystem that is continuously expanding and evolving.

Given all of that, it's understandable that we're going to make mistakes. Since awareness is always the first step in a long journey of discovery, let's take a moment to look coldly and clinically at four common mistakes we are making:

1. We tend to accept the client's view of the problem and we often assume the client's description of the problem is valid, accurate, and up to date without question.
2. We gravitate toward the first solution that seems reasonable, instead of choosing carefully among many possible solutions.
3. We don't align our solution with the client's overall strategic goals. As a result, our solution might work, but it doesn't ultimately help the client. (This is a version of the old joke "The operation was a success, but the patient died.")
4. We analyze data at the beginning and the end of campaigns, but tend to ignore or overlook data generated during campaigns. That can be a fatal mistake, since it makes it impossible to optimize campaigns on the fly.

And here are the four remedies:

1. Don't accept the client's viewpoint as gospel. Push back, consider the ecosystem, and find out what's really going on. I use this philosophy with my teams: If we can diagnose the client's problem, we can solve it.
2. Don't rush headlong into a solution just because it seems obvious. Resist the urge to act reflexively. In times of great change, an innovative solution will probably work better than a traditional approach.
3. Make sure you fully understand the client's business strategy and that your communication solution will actually help the client achieve its real-world business goals.
4. Start the "listening" process early. Collect data, analyze it, and learn how to use it. Don't wait for the client to come to you with a problem. If you're paying attention, you'll know what the problem is before the client tells you.

Above all, remember that any solution you devise will only work for a brief period of time. As an industry, we must get comfortable with the idea of continuous change. Dynamic engagement isn't just a fancy new term—it's a guiding principle, a mantra, and a road map.

In the chapters ahead, we'll share more stories and offer detailed solutions for handling the kinds of problems you'll face in our hyper-connected, always-on, data-driven, continuously evolving communication ecosystems. This will be an enjoyable ride—hang on!

KEY INSIGHTS

- The demands made by an "always on" world create a complex ecosystem of interconnected metrics, which get represented in brand reputation.
- Reputation arises from a complex system of interconnected brand management elements, situations, and events becoming the tangible proof of brand management efforts.
- The first impulse response to a reputation management challenge may not be the right one. The right response is made up of the sum of its parts, not controlled by one part. This is where data plays a key arbiter role in strategy development.
- Communication has to be dynamic, fluid, and in the moment, no longer a top-down process but instead a constant and transparent engagement between the customer and the brand.
- The new marketing team has to include web-savvy people, marketing people, social networking mavens, and data scientists, as well as liberal arts people, to engage all aspects of the conversation.

Note

1. This idea is commonly attributed to the pre-Socratic philosopher, Heraclitus of Ephesus, who was born roughly 2,500 years ago.

Chapter Two

Progress through the Revolutionary Storm: Why Data Science Matters

Executive Summary: Without a scientific methodology, Reputation Strategy becomes a patchwork of hunches and guesswork. While there is nothing inherently wrong with good old-fashioned human judgment, it can be augmented and strengthened through science. The speed at which information travels makes it virtually impossible to craft effective responses without understanding the full context of events and situations. Data science offers an objective perspective and provides a wider range of viable options for responding effectively to events that are beyond our control.

Taking an Iterative Approach

In his seminal book *Thinking, Fast and Slow,* Nobel laureate Daniel Kahneman writes that we have two psychological "systems" for responding to the problems we encounter in everyday life: "System 1" is the fast, instinctive response, while "System 2" is the slower, carefully considered response.

"System 1 operates automatically and quickly, with little or no effort and no sense of voluntary control," he writes. But System 2 requires conscious attention, intense focus, and studied concentration. We use System 1 to swerve quickly in traffic or detect an angry expression on someone's face. We use System 2 to balance our checkbooks or calculate the odds that we'll win a hand of blackjack.

Kahneman's basic theme resonates with me because it helps explain why data science has become an absolutely essential component of Reputation Strategy. Until very recently, it was possible to run a perfectly acceptable corporate communications operation on a rough blend of instinct and experience. In fact, the best practitioners were often the people with the "best gut feel" for dealing with an issue. As communications professionals, we were expected to leap into action at a moment's notice, and use our "superior" talents and abilities to eliminate or mitigate whatever problem had arisen.

As my friend and former colleague Marty Davis says, "Those days are gone. Today, you cannot control the conversation. You can respond effectively and try to make the situation better, but you cannot control it."

Marty has always been a great source of wisdom and advice, so let's take a moment to parse his words. From my perspective, you can't respond effectively to improve a situation unless you fully understand the context in which the situation occurred. In today's incredibly complex and multilayered communications ecosystem, data analytics are the best way for coming to grips with the shifting realities at play. I would argue that in the modern global economy, with all of its myriad dimensions and levels, there are no simple, one-size-fits-all solutions.

Data science is more than merely a new set of technologies—it's a way of looking at the world and embracing its complexity, diversity, and dynamism. It's the very opposite of a reductive approach that posits the existence of one solution for every problem. Instead of providing false hopes, data science offers a range of likely possibilities. From those possibilities, you make choices. Then you measure the results and tweak your plan accordingly. It's not guesswork—it's an iterative, scientific approach to a very difficult challenge.

Not a Replacement for Good Judgment

Someone recently asked me if it's possible to manage a Reputation Strategy without data analytics. I replied, "Yes, you can, but your strategy probably will not be very effective." Executing on Reputation Strategy is a lot like preparing a multicourse dinner for a large group of people: You need a menu, recipes, ingredients, utensils, bowls, pots, pans, a stove, an oven, and a dishwasher. Can you do it without all of those prerequisites? Sure, but you're asking for trouble!

That said, we still encounter pushback from people who think that data science somehow diminishes or denigrates the practice of communications. In fact, it has the opposite effect.

What we've discovered is that data science doesn't replace human judgment—it augments and empowers decision making. Instead of just guessing or playing a hunch, you get a range of options to choose among. For us, the primary advantage of a scientific approach is that it actually gives us a wider choice of actions. It provides a platform that encourages and supports experimentation. As a result, we aren't forced into putting all our eggs in one basket and hoping for the best outcome.

It is important to understand what data is telling you and to take the time to connect the dots in what you uncover in data and professional judgment and experience. In the case of reputation, data is often helpful to help us establish a "reputation baseline"; from that point there are other digital listening and monitoring tools that will help get a more complete picture of the broader environment in which the reputation exists.

Blending and Observing Data in Real Time

Data science also enables companies to view reputation on a much more granular level than ever before. From a practical perspective, that granularity allows you to see precisely which segments of a market are reacting or responding at any given time. Knowing who is saying what about your company—and when they are saying it—can make a huge difference in your decision-making process.

Not all deviations from the baseline require a full-scale response. With data science, you get a much more accurate picture of what's really going on, and you can decide among a range of practical options. Again, it's my belief that having a range of choices is better than being forced into some kind of simple binary decision that might not reflect the subtle realities of a particular situation.

We also factor in geopolitical risk analysis, which can be very helpful for narrowing down your options. No matter how much the world might seem like a "global village," location still plays a critical role in determining the appropriate response. An incident that occurs in Pittsburgh will require a different response from a similar incident in Phnom Penh or Peoria.

In addition to protecting your reputation, understanding geopolitical risk can help you protect your employees and your property. Some parts of the world are more volatile and less secure than other parts of the world. That doesn't mean you should stop doing business there, but you should have a methodology for assessing the risks on an ongoing basis. Data science can help you do exactly that.

Sometimes people ask me to explain the difference between business intelligence and data science. The answer is fairly easy: Business intelligence focuses on historical data, and as a result, it offers you a great view of the past. Data science, on the other hand, can be predictive. It combines historical and real-time data from multiple disparate sources. It enables you to analyze that data and search for patterns and anomalies.

Unlike traditional business intelligence, data science lets you look into the future. It doesn't give you a perfect view, but it can give you a fairly good idea of which outcomes are likely to occur and which aren't. That's the advantage of data science—it's forward looking. There's an old saying in the software industry that using business intelligence solutions to make decisions is like trying to drive your car by looking in the rearview mirror. That's a bit of an overstatement, but it makes the point.

You cannot control the past—it's already happened. But you can exert some influence over the future, for the simple reason that it's still in play. With the right set of predictive analytics and a good team of data scientists, you can reassert a measure of influence. Your influence might be more ephemeral than it was in the past, but we're not living in the past.

That's a hard message for many communications professionals to accept. The sooner we accept it, however, the sooner we can devise better ways for dealing with the needs of our clients. We're confident that there will always be a strong need for good communications strategy. The challenge is developing a new paradigm that works in a world that is both digitally connected and increasingly transparent.

Combining Data Science and Behavioral Economics

Data science and behavioral economics need to be combined to create effective Reputation Strategy practices for the real world. Data science is a critical tool for bringing objectivity in a highly complex and extremely fluid process.

In the past, you would identify a brand's stakeholders and then ask them to tell you about their expectations regarding that brand. There were two key problems with that approach. To begin with, it's very difficult for anyone to tell you what he or she wants you to become. Second, it's very difficult for a brand to become something different from what it already is.

It is also difficult to predict how customers would react to changes in a brand. Data science, and its ability to glean insights from large amounts of related and unrelated data generated from multiple sources, is an effective method of understanding and getting more value from data.

Separating signals from noise in the data is part science and part art.

Without data science, you're whistling in the dark. You can guess all you want, but if you want to really know whether a tactic or campaign is working effectively and generating value, you need data science.

Break Down the Silos

Many companies are hamstrung by their inability to analyze data that's sitting in multiple databases managed by various business units.

Getting data out of silos is also important because it often reveals that approaches that work for one business unit might not work for another unit. "This is critical in Reputation Strategy, because there's often a tendency to look for the one-size-fits-all solutions. In some cases, for example, the right answer might involve elevating trust through word of mouth. But that approach might not work in a different situation or at a different company. Data science helps us interpret the signals that indicate which approaches are working and which are not as effective.

Overcoming Big Data Fatigue

Another issue is perception. We've all heard and read so much about big data over the past decade that, quite frankly, many people have become bored with the topic. Some executives honestly believe the challenges of data have been solved, and they're ready to move on to something new.

The truth, however, is that we have only just begun to cross the frontiers of data science and predictive analytics. The combination of advanced data analytics and the Internet of Things (IoT) will surely drive huge transformations in the economy over the next two decades. We're not just talking about wearable exercise monitors and thermostats you can reset from your mobile phone—we're on the cusp of a revolution in which practically any device you can think of will have an IP address and will be connected to the Internet.

Those aren't merely blue-sky fantasies. Companies like Google, GE, IBM, Cisco, Microsoft, Intel, and Boeing are investing billions of dollars to develop the next generation of technologies required for a world of driverless cars, robotic airplanes, fully automated factories, hyper-efficient farms, and machinery that never breaks. A widely quoted Gartner report predicts the IoT will generate nearly $2 trillion in new value for the global economy over the next five years.[1]

It's not difficult to foresee a world in which every individual and every company is connected through the IoT. Imagine the impact on communications strategists when brands and their stakeholders are connected seamlessly across a truly universal multiplatform network like the IoT. If you think life is complicated today, just wait until tomorrow.

KEY INSIGHTS

- Brand management and Reputation Strategy are too complex for guesswork; a scientific approach is required that makes use of data from as many reliable sources as possible.
- Information that isn't shared quickly loses its value.
- Data that is relevant to reputation should be available to authorized users across the corporation and should not be kept in silos.
- Assumptions should be tested as scientifically as possible to determine which activities are most likely to produce optimal results and outcomes.
- As the quantities of data grow exponentially, a scientific approach to understanding what it tells us becomes increasingly crucial.
- Scientific data combined with behavioral analysis is the only way to manage the upcoming social changes like the Internet of Things. Technology is advancing at mega-speed; nothing will remain stagnant, nor should our methods of managing our Reputation Strategy.

Note

1. "Forecast: The Internet of Things, Worldwide, 2013," November 18, 2013, www.gartner.com/doc/2625419.

Chapter Three

The Digital Media Revolution Creates Completely New Business Models

Executive Summary: Digital media has brought communications and Reputation Strategy to a new level and shifted influence from the brand to the audience. Marketers and communications professionals need to learn the new rules of the road, and be mindful of which rules have changed and which rules remain the same.

E rin Byrne is managing partner, chief engagement officer at Grey Healthcare Group, one of the world's most respected health-care communications agencies. I've known Erin for nearly 20 years. From my perspective, she epitomizes the modern digital communications strategist. Erin is a leader and an innovator in social media, digital technology, corporate communications, and integrated marketing.

We sat down recently with Erin and asked her to describe the major differences between predigital and digital communications strategies.

"One of the biggest differences—and one of the most significant challenges—is the need to influence at a much different level. In the predigital era, your sphere of influence was smaller, but your ability as a brand to influence people directly was much greater," says Erin. "In many ways, the definition of influence has changed. It's become much more challenging for brands to identify the key influencers. Brands no longer have the control or the influence they had in the past."

I totally agree with Erin's take on this sea change. In the 1990s, it was really about getting a message directly to a stakeholder. The brand had much greater control over the dialogue. "Today, brands have very little control over the majority of the messages," says Erin. "Even when they do have some control, they can lose that control very quickly. Today, the voice of many can overtake the voice of the brand in an instant."

Erin has articulated a primary challenge facing communications strategists. Most of us work with brands that have grown their business by owning their message. That strategy is no longer operative, because it's virtually impossible for any brand to own or control its message. The balance of power has shifted dramatically—the audience controls the message. That simple fact creates a vast new universe of problems and opportunities for brands.

The good news is that digital natives—people who grew up surrounded by digital technologies—are joining the workforce and rising through the ranks to assume leadership roles at major brands and agencies.

"This new group of professionals will bring us to a new level," says Erin. "They're accustomed to more open dialogues between brands and their audiences. They understand how influence has shifted from brands to customers, and they seem comfortable with new rules of the road."

That doesn't mean that everything will be smooth sailing. It makes perfect sense that digital natives understand new technology and see it as an essential part of their lives. But do they also understand the need for integrated and coherent brand strategies, especially in a hyperconnected world?

"For the past 20 years, we've been figuring out how to apply technology to business. Now we're at the point where people understand technology, but they sometimes lack a clear understanding of how business works. I predict this will be a very exciting time for everyone," says Erin. "Some of the boxes we've lived in are being blown wide open."

For example, major brands such as Dove and McDonald's have run extremely successful campaigns with integrated messaging across multiple media platforms. Dove's campaign was founded on the premise that beauty is less a matter of physical appearance and more a matter of self-perception. The campaign was considered risky when it was launched, but has since proven wildly successful, propelling the brand from annual sales of $200 million to nearly $4 billion.

The Dove campaign worked because it focused more on the emotions of the audience than on the qualities of the products. Dove also relied heavily on a series of highly watchable videos to get its messages across. The videos were posted on YouTube and were viewed millions of times.

McDonald's is also a brand that knows how to use every available media channel to reach its audiences. Erin recalls her experience working on a McDonald's campaign several years ago: "They were being really attacked in the media about the nutritional value of their food. Our assignment was helping them change the public's perceptions. We built a program called Go Active, which was about helping people make better choices for themselves. McDonald's was doing its part by adding healthier menu options such as salads. But people also had to take responsibility for their choices."

The campaign involved creating a website called Goactive.com, Erin recalls. "It had a full exercise library and it gave you the ability to track your progress, along with all sorts of other health and wellness information to help you get there. Today, those kinds of sites are more common. But when we launched it in 2002, it was a very novel approach. The idea of a company truly wanting to contribute something of value to its audience and making an investment for the sake of its stakeholders was novel. Anyone with access to a computer could tap into the resources. It was a great example of using the web to amplify a positive message and spread it across a large audience. In a sense, the website became a community."

We asked Erin what advice she would offer to companies that are still wrestling with the complexities of the digital communications ecosystem. "First of all, some of the core principles of digital are not so different from core principles of traditional communications. Word of mouth, for example, is still very powerful," she said.

In the predigital era, you might typically hear about new products, new restaurants, or new movies from colleagues at work, friends on the softball team, or parents of children who played with your children. Today, brands can run word-of-mouth campaigns on many platforms ranging from social media to influencer marketing. "In the digital age, we have the potential to reach much larger audiences with word-of-mouth campaigns," says Erin. "Even though word of mouth is not a new idea, it can be scaled to a degree that simply was not possible before the arrival of digital media. For some brands, that's a hard concept to accept."

Brands also need to understand the importance of user-based design and user-based programming, says Erin. "They need to embrace the idea of contributing to their community. They need to know what makes their audience and their stakeholders unique. Then they can build programs and platforms that will be meaningful. It sounds simple, but it's a real challenge for many brands." And that contributing to their community represents their reputation.

Relational versus Transactional

Most brands reflexively want a product or service to be seen as "the solution" to a problem. But that's "a selfish perspective," says Erin, since it assumes there's a particular product that will fully address a customer's specific need. "Instead, brands should be figuring out how to address needs that are much broader and that can't be addressed by products alone," says Erin.

Let's say, for example, that a pharmaceutical brand is promoting a new smoking cessation product. One of the hard realities about smoking cessation is that a product—no matter how effective it is in lab tests—isn't usually enough to help smokers quit their smoking habit. "Medication alone won't do it," says Erin.

Instead of just launching the product and focusing on its excellent rate of success, the brand would also create an online community that provides smokers with tools and resources to support their efforts to stop smoking. In addition to providing a great product, the brand would also provide the motivation and encouragement that smokers need when they are struggling to overcome their habit.

Our conversation with Erin raised a great point that is often overlooked: Smart brands understand that it can be more important—and ultimately more profitable—to create meaningful relationships with customers and audiences, as opposed to merely trying to sell more products into the market. Smart brands see relationships, which can unfold and deepen over time, as more valuable than transactions, which tend to occur at single points of time.

A really smart brand would also open its smoking cessation program to any smoker who wants to quit, not just to those who choose the brand's product. "Because when anyone quits smoking, it's good for all of society," says Erin. Successful brands understand that it's not just about selling more products. Programs and initiatives that help the broader culture are great ways for brands to build up their reputations. And as Erin points out, it's far less burdensome to launch those kinds of efforts today than it was in the past.

"Even if you had wanted to create a program like that 50 years ago, it would have been very expensive and difficult to scale," says Erin. "Today, with mobile apps and web pages, you can create good programs quickly and cost effectively. That's a huge advantage."

Another difference is customization. In the past, an effective program would have likely required two or three brochures and other kinds of printed materials that could be assembled into a kit and mailed to participants. It would have been impractical and prohibitively expensive to create personalized kits for individual customers or groups of customers.

"Today, a segment can literally consist of one person," says Erin. "We can create a microsegment based on one person's needs and preferences, customized just for that person. That will be a major trend going forward."

Erin is a founding member of text4baby, an innovative free service that sends text messages with health tips and useful reminders to pregnant women and new mothers. "You sign up via text, enter your zip code and your due date," Erin explains. "Then you get three relevant targeted text messages per week. That kind of program for improving health outcomes wouldn't have been possible 25 years ago."

Indeed, text4baby is inarguably one of the best examples of how digital technology can be leveraged to serve legitimate social needs, efficiently and cost-effectively. A program like text4baby is especially useful for women in underserved communities, where there might be limited access to health care information through personal computers or laptops. "The opportunities for improving health through digital communication are very real and very exciting," says Erin.

Cognitive computing—the kind of computing pioneered at IBM for its Watson project—will also play a growing role in communications and Reputation Strategy. As Erin explains it, "We're at the very beginning of the cognitive computing age. We will increasingly use computers that can almost 'think' like humans, but at much faster speeds, and without all of our human biases and prejudices. Cognitive computing will revolutionize marketing and communications."

Erin also does volunteer work for the JED Foundation, a nonprofit organization dedicated to promoting emotional health and preventing suicide among college and university students. One of the challenges in preventing suicide is recognizing the warning signs and reaching out in time to save a person's life.

"Imagine if a computer like Watson could scan social media and look for signs of people at risk," says Erin. "Using techniques of contextual digital advertising, you could put a message in front of that person that might guide them to a suicide prevention hotline or a free counseling service. The potential for helping people is virtually limitless."

I admire Erin's thoughtful vision and her practical skill. As mentioned at the beginning of this chapter, people like Erin are the role models for the modern digital communications professional.

In any revolution, new business models often emerge. New approaches are created to meet the demands of the new normal. A brand's vitality lies in its capacity to endure and thrive in adverse times and in times of growth.

But don't lose heart. There is a discipline, a methodology for navigating the seeming chaos of the digital revolution that can help any organization on its road toward transformation, as shown in the following example.

Brand Essence Alignment It is easier said than done to ensure everyone really understands the brand's very essence. While many attributes can make up an overall brand profile, the reputation is often framed within a core essence: innovation or trust or speed to market. This is no academic distinction: the Reputation Strategy and resulting metrics emerge directly from these core values. Innovation might be measured in speed of new product sell-through, whereas trust might be measured in customer loyalty. Getting everyone on the same page early can ensure consistent execution downstream.

Reputation Strategy Once the brand essence is developed, the core metrics that will drive results are created within the Reputation Strategy. The data to manage a Reputation Strategy can provide early insights into competitive pressure or act as an early warning system suggesting weakness in future product adoption.

Governance The complexity of the always-on world requires a coordinated dance between data, operations, and sales. Governance provides the ground rules for improving results, line-of-sight responsibilities, and the data needed to generate success for everyone.

Capability Assessment It should not come as a surprise that in the fast-changing marketing world, the full capabilities of a communications organization may not be apparent. When there are all kinds of emerging channels—owned, earned, and paid—and they are fluid, the talent managing them should be able to do so in a fluid manner as well. The rigor of this step can save both time and money.

Implementation Road Map This is where the real magic happens, because one gets to knit together all the pieces—the data, the creative, the media, and the platforms. When properly engineered, the data provides the optimization layers that can, in real time, provide continuous improvement to live campaigns.

Performance Measurement To get measurements is relatively easy. To get performance metrics still remains tough for too many organizations. Too often, there are reams of data with every conceivable measure. Sometimes, a data diet is in order and you must limit yourself only to performance measurements. You may be happily surprised at the depth of data or you may be horrified at how tentative the data to sales dots can be. Either way, the learning will be instructive.

Risk Evaluation Risk is a word to strike fear into the heart of any manager. Yet a detached evaluation provides the objectivity to determine whether the risk is worth the potential reward.

Together, configuring a methodology that is appropriate for your organization's industry and ecosystem will, collectively, make the brand reputation stronger.

KEY INSIGHTS

- Digital media has completely and fundamentally transformed communications between brands and their audiences.
- Great brands focus on the strength and qualities of relationships; they see customers as "partners," not just as "consumers."
- New business models coordinate activities around data to provide a continuous set of indicators toward digital triumph of an always-on customer.

Chapter Four

Breaking the Branding Sound Barrier: The Role of Reputation Strategy

Executive Summary: Reputation is a strategy and strategies don't spring into existence overnight; they require thoughtful construction and attention to detail. Great branding is measured through a brand reputation that allows it to be resilient in all types of market conditions—from crisis to new breakthroughs. Great companies rely on their core principles, values, and beliefs. They don't rely solely on tactics; they use their "reputational equity" to weather the storm.

The Dark Matter of Marketing

Scientific theories abound about the abundance of the universe's "dark matter." Profound debates rage about its nature, volume, and the impact this invisible hand has on just about everything.

Successful brand management is tough because, much like mysterious dark matter, the brand is very much affected by a myriad of megaforces that fall outside the purview of brand management, such as CEO performance or a disruptive new entrant in the market. Within this very volatile environment, one can barely keep all the stars aligned, much less understand the interdependent nature of what one can see and the dark matter of marketing that one cannot see.

Why Reputation Matters

This is the primary value of a Reputation Strategy. It can be the guiding star shining a light on how all the variables contribute to or detract from the corporate brand. Through a rigorous set of dimensions that one can measure, reputation allows leaders to assess the overall behavior of the brand and its comparative performance over time.

By using reputation as the proof point of brand management programs, one can create sensitive measures that are meaningful. If, for example, the overall brand essence for a corporation is *trust,* then the reputation metrics will revolve around customer loyalty and customer satisfaction. Organizations with a product-centric brand essence will evaluate their reputation using new product adoption rates or user perception of products. With these tangible measures, reputation becomes a compass guiding the way through the mysterious channels of marketing and brand management.

One of my early mentors was Patrick "Pat" Ford, a corporate reputation and issues management specialist with more than 30 years of communications experience. Pat has consulted with a wide range of clients on corporate positioning, crisis and issues management, media relations, labor relations, and ally development.

He is currently the worldwide vice chair and chief client officer at Burson-Marsteller. Before joining Burson-Marsteller in 1989, he served as vice president for public affairs at the American Enterprise Institute for Public Policy Research in Washington, D.C. He began his career as a reporter for the *Jersey Journal* in Jersey City, New Jersey, and also served as a special New Jersey correspondent for Reuters. Pat was awarded the 2014 Milestones in Mentoring Legacy Award by the Planck Institute for Public Relations at the University of Alabama.

Our team sat down recently with Pat and asked him about his perspectives on the evolution of Reputation Strategy. Knowing Pat, I was confident his years of experience would be a valuable source of insight and that his stories would add a practical dimension to our book. Here is a condensed and lightly edited version of our conversation with him.

It's always important to have a strong Reputation Strategy in place. But in today's world, it's more important than ever because of the very high velocity at which events unfold—in the media, in the economy, in the environment around us—and that velocity is continually accelerating.

The fast pace of events poses ever-greater reputational risks— especially for companies and organizations that don't have a strong sense of their reputation and don't understand how best to protect it.

Reputation isn't just about what a company does. Reputation is also based on the manner in which a company operates. It's based on the character of its senior management, the quality of its products, how it behaves in communities where it operates, how it treats customers, treats investors, treats employees. Reputation involves every interaction and engagement with every stakeholder involved in the enterprise. The key word in all of that is "engagement."

There was a time when a lot of companies believed the process for building reputation began with inventing a clever tagline and then just spending a lot of money to buy advertising to build awareness around that clever tagline. But today's stakeholders— which include customers, investors, business partners, employees, and communities—expect much more than that now. They expect engagement. And most of them have access to some form of expression through the Internet, and so companies need to be engaged with every part of their stakeholder base. They need to do that on a continuing basis.

Not having a Reputation Strategy can hinder your ability to operate your business successfully. Moreover, you can find yourself at a disadvantage with pricing. The most famous example of this involved two different automakers, one American and one Japanese, using the same facility in the United States to manufacture automobiles. The automobiles were the same, except for the brand. The Japanese company was able to price its autos 15 percent higher than the American company—purely on the basis of reputation.

We asked Pat a follow-up question and his answer goes right to the heart of the matter.

In addition to the loss of pricing power, companies with less-than-stellar reputations have a harder time attracting employees, investors, and customers. Pat then raised another great point we hadn't previously considered in depth: What's the downside of not having a reputation? What happens when your reputation is neither good nor bad?

It's comforting to think that being "invisible" might confer some special advantage. But in real life, that isn't the way it works. One way or the other, problems will eventually arise. And when they do, having a great reputation can make all the difference. Here's a story Pat told us that illustrates the real value of a positive reputation.

A while ago, we were working with a company in Texas. It was a good company, but it had kept a low public profile. Nobody knew much about it. The company quietly decided to build a facility in a small East Texas town. Construction began, and the local community responded with an uproar of disapproval.

Although the company was virtually unknown, the towns-people assumed the worst. Suddenly, the company went from having no reputation to having a bad reputation!

The downside was that the company had to stop its construction and prepare a series of studies proving the new facility would be helpful rather than harmful to the surrounding community. The construction project was delayed and the company spent quite a bit of money mollifying the townspeople. On the positive side, however, the company learned an extremely valuable lesson. As a result of its experience in the small town, the company changed its procedures on a global basis. Now the company makes sure that whenever it launches a project, everyone who might be affected knows they're dealing with a thoroughly reputable company.

The takeaway here is that you can't assume being invisible provides you with a protective barrier. If you have no reputation, you're a blank slate. When something bad happens, people will project their worst fears onto you. It's fair to say that calming those fears will cost you money. So there's a real monetary value in having a great reputation. Pat compares reputation to financial equity and I totally agree with him.

Building Reputation over Time

Reputation is a form of equity. Like equity, you build reputation over time. You cannot simply spin it into existence overnight. You don't conjure it up with platitudes or slogans. You build it slowly, with demonstrated evidence that you are running a good business, making products that are good for the economy and good for people, and that you're creating jobs and keeping people employed. Eventually, when something bad happens, your reputational equity serves as a counterbalance.

People will accept explanations—when those explanations are tendered honestly. But honesty is often in the eye of the beholder. When the chips are down, a company with an existing reputation for honesty, integrity, and fair play will probably get the benefit of the doubt. Most people—particularly Americans—will forgive you if they feel you are truly contrite and completely honest. Here's how Pat explains that phenomenon.

> If there's one thing I've learned in this business, it's that people—whether they are customers, investors, employees, or citizens of a community—have a virtually unlimited capacity for understanding things can go wrong. Everyone understands that.
>
> If you're forthcoming about that and you are straightforward and admit what went wrong and you make amends and express concern for the people affected by it; demonstrate what you're doing to fix it; show how you're going to make sure that it doesn't happen again—chances are, especially if you've already got some of that equity built up that you can draw on, you're probably going to do fine.

But at the same time, people have almost zero tolerance for being manipulated or lied to or stonewalled. If you had any equity, you draw it down fast if you start to do any of those things. If you start to do those things and you haven't built any of that reputational equity, then you're probably in danger of ruining your business. It really is something that smart companies are very conscious of, especially in today's world.

Once upon a time, in the old days—maybe 10 to 15 years ago—when a problem would arise, one of the first things you did was try to contain it, and limit the damage to a local area.

Today, nothing is purely local. The Internet has largely obliterated the boundaries between local and global. It's also erased the boundaries between internal and external. The idea that you can keep something inside your company from becoming public is outdated. Those days are gone. Companies have to face up to reality and take steps to be transparent and authentic. Today, you've got to be real when you're dealing with your stakeholders.

The simple truth is that companies no longer control the message. All companies exist within an ecosystem. In the past, companies believed they could control the ecosystem. Clearly, that's no longer the case. You cannot simply "push out a message." You have to engage with stakeholders in a big, broad ecosystem. That's a very important realization about how the global economy works. It isn't one company or one country against the rest of the world or trying to dominate the world. It's one big collaborative system. If you're going to compete successfully in that system, you'll need a clear sense of mission and a strong reputation.

We asked Pat for his take on the difference between crisis management and Reputation Strategy. His response was instructive.

To me, they're really two different things. Effective crisis management is one element within a Reputation Strategy. Crisis management is necessary, because crises can happen anywhere at any time. There are things beyond your control that are going to arise in the course of doing business. But ideally, you want to deal with them before they become full-blown crises.

But this ties into the overarching importance of Reputation Strategy. Because in many cases, the real crisis results not from the fact something happened, but from how a company reacted to whatever it was that happened. In other words, it's not always the event itself that provokes the crisis. Sometimes it's the response: It's how you react, or how you don't react.

Boots on the Ground

Before leaving this chapter, I want to share one more of Pat's stories. I found this story particularly useful, because it illustrates the value of being present when a situation is unfolding. The year was 2002, and the client was a major steel company. Here's a summary of how the events unfolded, based on Patrick's recollections.

The client was one of two companies seeking to acquire four steel mills owned by another steel company that was in bankruptcy court. We quickly realized the most important factor wasn't legal or financial—it was reputational.

The bankruptcy judge had to determine which deal was best—the deal offered by our client or by one of its competitors. More was at stake than dollars—the jobs of hundreds of employees, along with their pensions, were also at risk. It would have been easy for the judge to focus on the negatives and simply favor the company making the highest dollar offer.

We based our communication strategy on our client's longstanding reputation as a sturdy pillar of the U.S. economy. We focused on what would be gained from the deal—and how the communities around the four steel mills would benefit. We focused on our client's traditional role in the domestic steel industry, and the importance of preserving the industry for future generations.

We developed a set of core messages around the theme that while the acquisition wasn't the ideal outcome, it was the best possible outcome and held the most promise for the communities around the four steel mills.

Those messages were delivered in person by our client's representatives—the folks who would actually be managing the plants—at meetings with local business, church, and citizen groups in each of the four communities over several months.

Despite a higher bid from the competing steel company, the bankruptcy court awarded those facilities to our client. The United Steelworkers, which was one of the largest creditors in the bankruptcy proceedings, also gave its strong endorsement to the decision. The court's decision really demonstrates the value of our client's reputation.

I really appreciate the "boots on the ground" aspect of this story. The client company sent its managers to the communities to make the case in person. Today, many people tend to think of Reputation Strategy as something that happens in digital domains, but the communication ecosystem is still rooted firmly in the physical world and it's critical not to overlook the value of a good neighbor-to-neighbor campaign.

Several times in our conversation, Pat mentioned the importance of falling back on core principles in times of difficulty. That is extremely valuable advice. As Pat once said to me, "You want to board up your windows before the hurricane hits, not while it's hitting you."

From our perspective, Reputation Strategy begins with a clear sense of mission and purpose. The next step is developing a thorough and objective understanding of your stakeholders. You need to know who cares about what you do, who is affected by your actions, and who is capable of influencing the opinions and feelings that other people have about your organization.

We'll return to the idea of stakeholder mapping in a subsequent chapter. Pat reminded us in our conversation that, for many companies, the idea of stakeholder mapping seems daunting. But in reality, it's a necessary exercise and it's usually not as hard as it initially seems.

As we've discussed earlier, sometimes there are fewer people or groups involved than you initially imagined. In many cases, what seems like "everybody" turns out to be a handful of influential people. That said, you still need a Reputation Strategy—because sometimes it's easier to persuade millions of people to trust you than it is to persuade one or two people to trust you.

KEY INSIGHTS

- Reputation is the proof point of a well-executed brand and long-term corporate strategy.
- It's important to understand the concerns and interests of stakeholders at every level of the conversation.
- The way a company or brand responds to a crisis is absolutely critical; a poorly conceived response can make a bad situation worse. A well-conceived response can result in brand loyalty even in difficult times for the brand.
- A positive reputation is achieved by demonstrating transparency, honesty, and an awareness of the concerns of all the people.
- Companies no longer control the conversations around their reputations, so it behooves companies to ensure a good reputation through transparency, honesty, and an awareness of the concerns of all the people involved in any transaction.

Chapter Five

Reputation and Your Brand's DNA

Executive Summary: The best reputation strategies often begin before a product launch. Today, it's normal for audiences to expect high levels of transparency and engagement from brands. Sometimes over-sharing information about your products is a better strategy than under-sharing information. Let the audience decide how much information is too much.

I s it possible to front-load reputation during a launch? Can you build reputation into a brand's DNA? How much value does a great reputation really confer on a brand in today's hyperactive markets? In an age of total transparency, can brands afford to hide or conceal information?

Those were some of the questions we were asking ourselves before our conversation with Ame Wadler, a good friend and former colleague. Ame has more than 25 years of experience in public relations and public affairs. Her career spans long stints at Hill and Knowlton, Edelman Worldwide, and Burson-Marsteller. She's played leading roles in more than 20 biopharmaceutical launches, including more than 10 blockbusters.

Our research team interviewed Ame and asked her to describe how Reputation Strategy has become more complicated and more nuanced over the past two decades.

> "There's no question that Reputation Strategy has changed enor-mously, and there have been two primary drivers: The audience's expectations have changed and how we interact with an audience has changed," Ame says. "In the past, most of the audience was from the so-called silent generation. They were accustomed to a com-munications style that was more top-down. Today's audiences— younger Baby Boomers, Millennials, Gen Xers—expect transpar-ency. They expect their opinions to count and they expect to play a role in shaping how companies communicate with them. Today you have audiences whose expectations are completely different from audiences of the past, and as a result, the older styles of com-municating just don't carry the same weight they used to."

In our conversation, Ame spoke about the rising value of owned media—content that is created or curated by a brand and disseminated through its websites and various social-feed platforms. I believe that owned media is an area of opportunity that's overlooked by many brands and their agencies. I'm not putting down earned media and paid media; they still bring lots of value to the table. But it's time for all of us to look more closely at owned media as a potential game changer in today's complex communications ecosystems.

> "Today we are all publishers and producers. We all have the channels to reach people directly. Owned media can be an exceptionally valuable tool, and being able to use it effectively is really an art," says Ame.

Can owned media create the risk of appearing self-congratulatory or less credible? Yes, but only if you confuse it with public relations. Ame says it's all about creating context.

> Owned media doesn't mean only telling your stories, but tell-ing stories that are relevant to your stakeholders and ... curating content from other thought leaders and other influencers who

are maybe not telling your story directly, but who have related stories that support your brand.

So when you tell your own specific story, you're telling it within the context of many, many other stories that you are curating and sharing. And when you have an issue, you have that much more credibility but you also have the vehicle already engaging people to allow you to tell that story.

But the idea is that you don't just deploy it when you have a problem or when you're launching the brand. You deploy it all the time and you have an editor dedicated to it. Whether the editor is somebody on your staff or working for your agency, it's a full-time job.

Reflecting on Ame's words, I was struck by how much the world has changed in such an astonishingly brief span of time. The Internet, the World Wide Web, social media, and broadband mobile connectivity have totally transformed the way all of us relate to one another. It's not surprising that the ways companies and brands relate to their audiences have also changed and evolved—but the incredibly fast pace of those changes seems breathtaking. Ame went on to talk about current expectations in communication.

We've moved from a relatively static nine-to-five news cycle to a highly dynamic 24/7 news environment that often changes minute by minute. The idea that you can release a statement and that's the end of the conversation is naive. Social media gives everybody a voice. People expect companies to engage with them and to listen to their opinions. They expect a level of transparency that's never existed before.

In the "good old days," a communications professional had a Rolodex with the names and telephone numbers of reporters. When a company or an organization needed to communicate with its audience, the standard practice was picking up the phone and calling a reporter. Today, the typical communications pro is more likely to tweet a quick message to a blogger and hope the blogger responds by writing a post that can be shared on Twitter, Tumblr, Facebook, and other social platforms.

New Times Demand New Ideas

Talking about the role of reputation management is easy, but creating the operational muscle behind the talk is the not-so-easy part. The way to start is to introduce a defined process that drives toward Reputation Strategy alignment.

Put Your Best Foot Forward

We also asked Ame to talk about the key lessons she learned over a long career of launching new brands and products and its impact on Reputation Strategy. Characteristically modest, her answers were helpful and generous.

> I've been really fortunate ... I've been able to work with many great brands. The advice I give to companies is "be authentic." You hear the word "authentic" a lot, but it's not that easy and you can't fake it. For me, the programs that have been most successful are those programs where there is a "north star" for all communications. The "north star" is what the company stands for.

Figure 5.1 The Process for Integrating Reputation Strategy into Corporate DNA

The "north star" that Ame mentions serves as a set of guiding principles for communicating with audiences. It creates what Ame describes as a sense of unity or seamlessness between a company's internal and external behaviors. When you have a "north star," everything related to communications becomes a lot easier—whether it's a new product launch, a product recall, a change in leadership, a new program, or an unexpected crisis.

> I actually think it's a little bit less about communications in some cases and more about behavior. The good news is that most companies do behave the right way. But they don't always recognize that they need to talk about how they behave. Sometimes an organization does all the right things, but isn't recognized for its accomplishments. Usually when that happens it's because the organization is afraid that people won't think they're doing enough. Some organizations create false barriers that prevent them from talking about their achievements. Most of the time, those barriers aren't real; they're imaginary. It's all about your mindset. You have to be proud of who you are and what you are doing.

The launch of Lipitor in 1997 is a great example of how a brand can overcome uncertainty by putting the best available information in front of the public. When Lipitor was launched, there were already four similar medicines on the market and many people, including doctors, didn't fully understand the potential benefits of lowering LDL cholesterol. Some people questioned whether the world really needed a fifth cholesterol-lowering drug. It took a leap of faith—and a brilliantly managed educational marketing campaign that included ads on the popular TV program *ER*—to convince people that Lipitor's ability to reduce "bad" cholesterol" more dramatically than similar drugs made it worth trying.

Linda A. Johnson, a business writer who covers pharmaceuticals, biotech, and hospitals for the Associated Press, wrote an excellent article in 2011 that recaps the story of Lipitor's rise from an also-ran to the world's top-selling drug. In her article, Johnson explains how Lipitor was invented at Warner-Lambert, which then partnered with Pfizer to run additional studies and create a world-class marketing campaign. Pfizer eventually bought Warner-Lambert and went on to conduct "more than 400 studies, costing roughly $1 billion and including more than 80,000 patients. The studies have shown how Lipitor helped patients with heart problems, diabetes, stroke risk, and other conditions, by preventing heart attacks and strokes and reducing plaque buildup in arteries."[1]

Pfizer's willingness to share its information certainly contributed to the public acceptance and spectacular success of Lipitor. From my perspective, it's a valuable lesson in the value of "putting your best foot forward" and sharing data that supports your cause. As Ame suggested earlier, it makes little sense to erect imaginary boundaries between your brand and its audiences.

Customers Reward Brands That Share Information

Another excellent example where Reputation Strategy was paramount was Ame's description of the launch of a biologic prescription medicine for treating chronic diseases.

> It was one of the very first of the biologics, which are genetically engineered medicines. It changed the way people would get treated. We were moving into a new territory and there were many unknowns. Early on, we put together a group of patients, their family members, and the people who cared for them. We brought them together to keep us straight about what we knew and what we didn't know. They helped us set the tone for all of our communications moving forward.
>
> We kept inviting new people into that group. . . . Eventually we had 200 patients and their caregivers . . . who would continue to keep us honest about how we were communicating and let us know whether our educational programs were truly educational. We would engage with them on a very consistent basis. They told us what was important to them and what wasn't. Even as we had great science to report, we knew that we had to share it in a way that would be useful for physicians and also useful for patients. Because we asked them from the very beginning and because we followed their guidance, the patients and their caregivers trusted us.

The bond of trust between the patients and the drug's manufacturer proved its value during a period of time when it became difficult to produce the drug in large enough quantities to meet the demand. As Ame explained to our team, biologics are inherently difficult to make. "If a batch goes wrong, you could end up with a supply issue and patients can't get the medication they need," Ame says. When situations like that occur, physicians will often prescribe an alternative drug.

Because the group of patients and caregivers trusted the drug and trusted the company, they didn't switch to another drug when supply issues occurred. "They rallied each other to hold on and they supported each other," Ame says. As a result of that long-term trust, short-term supply issues did not escalate into full-blown disasters.

> We took great pride in our ability to engage with people, to listen to them, and to learn from them. People need to know they're being heard and respected. To me, that drives reputation. But listening to people is hard because what you hear often flies in the face of what you were taught in school or what your marketing research is telling you. We learned that your willingness to listen and your reputation are deeply connected.

We also asked Ame to list some of the most common mistakes she sees companies make when trying to safeguard their reputations. Again, her replies were insightful and instructive.

> The first and foremost mistake is defensiveness. Most companies should start from the premise that they're doing the best that they can, and when they make mistakes, they need to own them. Instead of being defensive, they should be explanatory. Generally, my advice is to explain your mistakes rather than trying to defend them. Show people what you're doing to correct your mistakes, show them your accomplishments, and acknowledge that even if you're not 100 percent there yet, you're doing everything you can, as quickly as you can, to fix the problem.
>
> This next mistake always makes me cringe: when a company executive or spokesperson doesn't answer the question that's being asked. Okay, we've all been through media training and we know how to bridge. But bridging doesn't mean ignoring.

You need to listen to the question and answer it, or you'll come off as evasive.

Another common mistake is trying to talk in sound bites. When you do that, you risk sounding glib. You lose the context and richness of regular speech. Brevity shouldn't force you to limit the depth or the context of what you're trying to say.

Finally, there are many companies that simply don't know how to say "I'm sorry." Saying "I'm sorry" can prevent a lot of pain. Sometimes, people just need to hear you say, "I'm sorry." It sounds like a kindergarten thing, but it can be extremely important to your brand.

Toward the end of our conversation, we asked Ame to suggest four positive steps that every brand should take to build and safeguard its reputation. Here are her four suggestions.

1. *Know yourself.* Know what you've done well. Know what you could do better and own it. Until you've done that, you don't have a good story to tell.
2. *Listen.* Respond to what you hear in a way that is natural for you and consistent with your organization's ethos. Then listen again.
3. *Ask questions.* Did we give you what you needed? Are we still giving you what you need? Do you need more? What more can we be doing for you?
4. *Don't overpromise.* If you deliver on your promises, you're doing okay. If you overdeliver, you're a hero. But if you don't deliver on what you say you were going to deliver, people will stop believing you and then whatever road you travel will be full of potholes.

KEY INSIGHTS

- In many situations, owned media can be the best investment and involves careful data-driven integration with paid and earned channels.
- Know your brand's "north star" and let it guide all of your brand's communications expressed and measured in the brand's Reputation Strategy operating model.

- Creating strong bonds of trust between a brand and groups of loyal customers can help the brand weather reputational crises.
- At great brands, external and internal behaviors are essentially the same; great brands usually have a strong set of operating principles and carefully defined core beliefs that guide behaviors and continually enhance reputation.
- Engage with your product buyers and establish a working relationship so that they feel they are a part of the business. They will pay a premium for a product when they feel they are being engaged with and heard.
- Be honest and direct.
- Know your strengths and accomplishments and don't be afraid to make them known.
- Customers want to feel an "intimacy" with the brand, so err on the side of giving too much information, rather than withholding. Let the customers decide how much information they want.

Note

1. Associated Press, "Lipitor Becomes World's Top-Selling Drug," Crain's New York Business, December 28, 2011, www.crainsnewyork.com/article/20111228/HEALTH_CARE/111229902/lipitor-becomes-worlds-top-selling-drug.

Chapter Six

The Economics of Reputation

Executive Summary: In modern competitive markets, reputation has business value and should be treated as an asset. Measuring reputation should not be a "one shot" exercise, but a consistent process performed diligently at regular intervals. It's a good practice to establish a baseline from which subsequent measures can be compared. Having a baseline makes it easier to spot trends and emerging patterns that can be used by the organization to improve performance and mitigate risk.

For this chapter, I sought to answer the question I get so often from colleagues and clients asking about the economic value of reputation. And in particular, is there something that we, as communications practitioners, need to be doing differently given the changes in how companies are using social and digital channels to engage with stakeholders.

Most people understand that reputation has economic value. The challenge is determining the type and amount of its value to your organization. Reputation can be a strategic imperative, but as an economic contributor, its value will vary by industry and by company. In some industries, reputation will account for more than in other industries. It is important to understand how reputation affects your industry and your enterprise.

The potential impact of reputation on the economic health of the modern enterprise requires a nontraditional and unconventional approach. Practitioners today must rethink the traditional idea that reputation is a subset of a public relations strategy or a subsidiary function of a corporate communications department. In keeping with the theme of this book, it also means taking a scientific approach to the concept of reputation.

Historically, companies hire a market research firm or they commission a survey that measures reputation at a specific moment in time. That's not the right way to measure reputation, especially when you believe that it has real economic value. Imagine if your CFO looked only at sales data from a single day instead of from an entire quarter or year. Imagine if the CFO looked only at the most current sales data, and didn't compare it to sales data from the previous quarter and previous year. That would never happen in a modern enterprise.

Traditionally, reputation has been measured in snapshots of time that do not tell a complete story. If we are going to treat reputation as a strategic contributor to business, then we need to find a better and more rigorous way to measure it. And we definitely need to measure it consistently over a period of time, not just in quick intervals.

Consistent measurement over time certainly suggests the need for a practical framework and a set of processes designed to generate usable data that can be analyzed to produce actionable insights for the organization. For example, you'll want to know how your reputation has been trending over the past 12 months, whether the trends are positive or negative, and how the trends are influencing your company's performance relative to its competitors.

Reputation: An Asset of Increasing Value

Is it fair to categorize reputation as an asset? I recall debating this topic with the CFO of a Fortune 50 company in the last few years. The discussion got tense because I was arguing about the economic impact of data with very little evidence to support my claims. I strongly believe that reputation is and should be categorized as an asset. But I do not think companies need to put it on a balance sheet along with other tangible assets. Reputation and its importance to organizations is increasing in significance and becoming more tangible.

Every year, companies develop sharper and more accurate methods and technologies for measuring performance and value across their lines of business. As we improve our ability to track and measure the most subtle indicators of performance, reputation will become as tangible as many of the other business metrics we now consider critical to gauging the health of the modern enterprise.

For those who would still argue the value of reputation, I suggest considering the negative impact of a poor reputation. In a market economy, sellers compete for the attention of buyers. When you have a bad reputation, it is much harder to attract buyers. Instead of being an asset, your reputation becomes a liability.

A bad reputation can lead to a loss of pricing power, particularly when a company is competing against firms with better reputations. Major customer brands learned many years ago that pricing power is directly proportional to reputation—the more people like you, the more they're willing to pay a higher price for your products.

A bad reputation can be a slippery slope—or as one of my friends used to say, "One bad thing leads to another." Let's take a hypothetical example: A large company with a reputation for treating its customers poorly tries to acquire a competitor. The proposed acquisition raises some antitrust concerns among government regulators, but what ultimately sinks the deal is the public outcry from the company's customers. Using traditional and social media, the customers persuade the regulators to look more closely at the acquisition. Facing months of scrutiny from regulators *and* a barrage of negative publicity, the company abandons the plan to acquire its competitor.

In that hypothetical case, the company's reputation was pure dead weight. I'm sure you can think of examples from real life in which you quietly—or perhaps not so quietly—rooted against a company that had mistreated you or someone you know.

In my experience, brands get into trouble when they start acting like monopolies and they forget that customers have choices. In today's high velocity economy, there seems to be no scarcity of choices for customers. New products and new services are introduced every day. Markets are growing in size, diversity, and complexity. Barring a zombie apocalypse, I don't see that trend reversing itself anytime soon. The competition for customers will continue to intensify—and that means reputation will become more important than ever before.

A Competitive Factor

One effective way of measuring reputation is through a competitive lens. You can assess your reputation against another company in a similar business or selling similar products. If you look at their sales and pricing data and compare those numbers to your numbers, reputation will likely be a factor of difference, especially as it relates to consumer choice, intent to purchase, and loyalty.

How much of a difference reputation makes is the big question. The difference will vary by industry, by market, and by company. What's important is that companies take the steps necessary to quantify the value of reputation. That's the only way to know for sure.

Many professionals recommend developing a baseline measure that you can use to determine the impact of reputation on performance over time. I fully agree. Modern data science provides many techniques and processes for collecting and analyzing data from multiple internal sources and blending it with data from multiple external sources to produce information that can be used to improve performance in both the short and long term.

Much of the data you need for a competitive analysis is already being collected. The goal now is taking the data you already have and integrating it with other data from additional sources. Then you can analyze it relative to your baseline and really begin to see how reputation affects your performance.

You can expect your baseline measure to change over time. Every company will have a different set of metrics to guide its Reputation Strategy. Choosing the right metrics will become an essential leadership skill.

In some situations, revenue and profit will weigh more heavily than other metrics. But as markets become more interconnected and supply chains become more complicated, a more nuanced set of metrics might be necessary. Again, this is where the ability to gather, integrate, and rapidly analyze data from multiple sources becomes essential.

In Pursuit of "Perfect Information"

Big data offers us greater transparency despite protestations that we are "drowning" in data. The truth is that quick access to huge amounts of information has already transformed our lives in many positive ways.

From the perspective of the typical customer—and all of us are typical customers to one degree or another—access to more information has shifted the advantage from the seller to the buyer. We don't have to rely on a sales rep's promise that a product is great—we can look it up and find out what a million other customers think about the product. Thanks to information, we have choices and options that we never had before.

Many pundits said the flood of data would result in a paralyzing "information glut" that would make life harder for customers and ordinary citizens. I contend that it has done just the opposite. Today, we live in a world of nearly "perfect information." By "perfect information," I mean vast amounts of reliable information gathered from multiple sources that you can access with minimal effort to support your decision-making processes.

For example, a friend was recently apartment hunting in Brooklyn. Something about the rental agent made her suspicious, and she looked up his company's background on her mobile phone. Within 30 seconds, she knew that numerous complaints and lawsuits had been filed against the company. She cut short her appointment with the agent, and found a more reliable company to help her find an apartment. The entire process didn't take days or weeks—it took minutes.

Itamar Simonson and Emanuel Rosen have written an interesting book, *Absolute Value: What Really Influences Customers in the Age of (Nearly) Perfect Information,* in which they examine how access to information has radically altered relationships between buyers and sellers. The authors use the term "absolute value" to denote the quality of a product as experienced by the people who actually buy it.

By reading or hearing about the experiences of other people who have purchased the same product or similar products, prospective buyers can do a better job of predicting whether the product they intend to buy will actually meet their expectations. Customers equipped with "perfect information" tend to ignore marketing messages and focus instead on the experiences of other customers. In a sense, customers are becoming less emotional and more rational in their decision-making processes.

"When we talk about absolute value, we are not talking about some universal truth about a product for a certain customer. . . . We're referring to a customer's ability to get closer to knowing her likely experience with a product," the authors write.

The good news is that forewarned is forearmed. Brands can take advantage of this shift in customer behavior in several ways. First, brands can concentrate more of their resources on creating products that deliver the experiences that customers actually want. Second, brands can tweak their messages to emphasize rational reasons to buy, instead of relying primarily on emotional appeals. Third, brands can bring new products to market faster and with more confidence because they'll be able to find out almost immediately if the products are hits or misses.

"When quality can be quickly assessed, people are less hesitant to try something new," according to the authors. For brands, that translates into lower costs for introducing new products or entering new markets, and quicker time to turn around perceived problems in a product.

The moral is that data and information don't work exclusively for buyers or for sellers. They are inherently neutral. It doesn't matter whether you are a brand or a customer—the information you need to make better decisions is available and waiting for you to use it.

Who Owns Reputation?

I am often asked the question "Which department or area of the corporation should be responsible for reputation?" Most of us agree that reputation can be a strategic factor, and that it can play a significant role in the eventual success or failure of an enterprise. We're less certain about who should be held accountable for reputation. Some people I know think the chief marketing officer should "own" reputation. Others believe strongly that it should rest with the chief financial officer or the chief risk officer. Recently, some have suggested the creation of a new executive role, the chief reputation officer.

At the risk of sounding overly simplistic, I think that reputation is everyone's responsibility. Companies that care about their reputation should have written policies explaining the value of reputation and why it needs to be protected. Every corporate officer, executive, manager, employee, and consultant should be trained to understand the company's policy on reputation, and there should be clear processes for managing reputational issues when they arise.

The net takeaway here is straightforward: Reputation has economic value and it should be treated as a tangible strategic asset. Smart companies, in my estimation, will take the time and devote the resources necessary to develop practical frameworks and standard processes for building, enhancing, and preserving their reputation.

Reputation, Risk, and Creating Opportunity

It's axiomatic that risk and profit are linked—you can't have one without the other. Where there is risk, there is also opportunity. Our experiences in the marketplace have taught us that reputation poses risks and opportunities.

Great brands are mindful of both possibilities. In the detailed case study in Chapter 12, you'll find a step-by-step description of a strategic reputation campaign. In that chapter, we elaborate on our belief that reputation is more than just a risk factor—it is also a competitive advantage that should guide business decisions.

Brands that integrate qualitative and quantitative data, primary research, regression analysis, and digital listening to generate meaningful insights not only do a better job of protecting their reputations—they also leverage their reputation capital to create opportunities for strategic growth.

Before leaving this topic, I want to touch briefly on a related area. To an increasing degree, risk management depends on Reputation Strategy.

For that reason, I thought it would be good to include a short interview with Yasmin Crowther, chief of strategy and research at Polecat, a big data and digital intelligence firm founded in 2007 by two former Microsoft executives. Polecat provides advanced digital analytics and intelligence to many of the world's leading corporations and consultancies. We posed several questions to Yasmin and here are her responses, condensed and lightly edited.

Question: *From your perspective, what's the value of reputation in a networked global economy?*

Answer: As companies in some instances outstrip the GDP and reach of small states, there is commensurate need for great care in how they shepherd their resources, impact, and reputation. The court of public opinion can be at least as harsh as courts of law. Successful companies tend to be those that can demonstrate the value they deliver to society—as well as to shareholders—and who deliver transparency and accountability for both the risks and opportunities accrued as a result of their business practices.

Question: *What's the relationship between reputation economics and data analytics?*

Answer: Data-driven analytics allow companies to take a good, hard look at the digital footprint surrounding their performance and that of their peers—what matters to the rest of the world; the degree of contentiousness and hostility; leaders and laggards. Analytics intrinsically challenges any corporate tendencies to myopia and holds up the mirror of the world—good, bad, and ugly. The corporate choice of how to engage and respond is fascinating and I'm sure will play a part in defining the world's most successful future brands.

Question: *What's the best way of explaining the value of risk intelligence to modern brands and their executives?*

Answer: Most execs (those worth their salt) who look after brands understand that the success of their brand is defined (in whole or in part) by how it deals with contentious issues and stakeholders. A diverse range of companies—from Shell to Nike, Starbucks, Wal-Mart, and Apple—have dealt with serious risks to their brand and business, with the most successful working to transform those risks into opportunities. Analytics profoundly enhance business intelligence and the ability to understand—and, critically, to anticipate—diverse concerns, risks, and opportunities.

Question: *What's the link or connection between risk intelligence and Reputation Strategy?*

Answer: The fundamental challenge is that companies need to understand how diverse stakeholders regard and affect their business, while also keeping an ever-watchful eye on the increasingly exposed nature of their entire value chains, be it a Swiss subsidiary or a garment factory in Bangladesh. You can't have a Reputation Strategy that isn't as smart as possible to current and emerging risks—and the opportunities and liabilities therein. Analytics allow companies to be better informed about their stakeholders and also the digital footprint of their own value chains and key markets.

We also asked Yasmin to share some of her favorite examples of how a scientific approach to risk intelligence helped companies avert or minimize damage from unforeseen events.

A major energy company—in the wake of an environmental catastrophe—engaged with priority stakeholders in key markets to understand their perceptions and expectations. As well as face-to-face engagement with investors and NGOs, they used digital analytics to help understand and demonstrate the balance and polarization of opinions and needs in different geographies. The fact that the company could bring this holistic context and analysis to the table helped inform direct engagement and mitigate against overly personalized opinions and polarization.

Another energy company is using analytics to inform its climate change strategy in the run-up to COP21 in Paris. The analytics will help the company understand how regulatory conversations differ from broader societal and social media concerns, and to inform the nature of its own interventions and issue management.

KEY INSIGHTS

- Reputation creates economic value for the enterprise and should be treated as an asset.
- Reputation has strategic value, which suggests that it should be part of board-level discussions.
- Risk management and risk intelligence processes are integral to Reputation Strategy in rapidly evolving modern markets.
- The safeguarding and proponents of relationship management must be part of the corporate culture, and responsibility belongs across all company levels.
- Data analytics can give a clear view of what exactly is going on in different geographies, in specific business lines, and among various customer groups. More than just a static snapshot of reputation, analytics are crucial to show trends, guiding brand executives and action plans.
- The speed of today's communications can work in the company's favor by which messages can be repurposed to provide instant feedback on products and strategies. This can deliver better insights to optimize investments.

Chapter Seven

Co-Creation Is Essential for Aligning Brands and Customers

Executive Summary: Smartphones and mobile tablets are game-changers. Managing relationships between brands and their markets requires strategies and structures that are nuanced, disciplined, and antifragile. Co-creation is essential for aligning brand communications with the interests and values of your audience.

Communication strategies exist for the purpose of developing, supporting, growing, and sustaining brands in competitive markets. Since it is virtually impossible to talk meaningfully about Reputation Strategy without also talking about brand strategy, let's dive right in.

Brand strategy has numerous components and moving parts. Rather than focusing on operational tactics, it's helpful to look at the basic conceptual elements that form modern brand strategies. First, let's clear up a misconception that *interacting* with customers is equivalent to *engaging* with customers. You can interact with anybody at any time. Engaging with someone implies a degree of permission, which requires a preexisting relationship. Are you beginning to sense a hierarchy?

Imagine a Maslow-type pyramid (see Figure 7.1) with customer experience at the base. For all brands, large and small, the most basic requirement is providing customers with satisfactory experiences. If you can't do that, your brand is kaput.

The creative team at Boston-based Black Coffee said it best by asserting that brands are experiences that sit at the intersection of an expectation and a promise. The customer provides the expectation and the brand supplies the promise. When the expectation and the promise match up, the result is a positive experience, increasing the brand's reputation.

Generating a series of consistently positive experiences isn't easy, but it's a basic requirement of staying in business. Contrary to popular belief, technology doesn't always make it easier for brands to thrive. The same

Figure 7.1   Modern Brand Strategy Pyramid

cool technologies that make it easier for a brand to deliver their products and services quickly and profitably also make it easier for customers to switch brands without losing a beat. Customer loyalty isn't dead; it just isn't what it used to be. Smartphones and other mobile devices give customers the power to opt in and out of brands with a touch or a swipe, from any location—assuming there's a signal, of course!

Relationships Still Matter

Brands that consistently provide positive experiences can move up to the pyramid's next level, which is building relationships. Customer relationships are exceedingly valuable because they engender feelings of familiarity and trust. When your customers trust you, they're much more open and receptive to your message.

The next level up on the pyramid is engagement. Yes, the word "engagement" has been overused and misused, but it's still a critical component of brand strategy and we cannot ignore it. Here's why: Engagement happens when customers feel less like passive customers and more like active partners in productive relationships. From my perspective, engagement is absolutely essential to the next step, which is loyalty.

When I began my career, customer loyalty was the ultimate goal, the nirvana of brand strategy. It was like reaching the summit of Mount Everest and winning the Super Bowl.

Customer loyalty meant predictable recurring revenues, less churn, and lower marketing costs—because it's generally less expensive to retain loyal customers than it is to acquire new customers.

Shared and Aligned Values

Loyalty is also a true test of a brand's relationships with its audience, because it depends on a set of shared and aligned values that embody the reputation of the brand. Loyalty is the audience's way of saying, "Hey, we're on the same page. We believe in what your brand represents."

I highly recommend reading "Three Myths about What Customers Want,"[1] a short post on the HBR Blog Network by Karen Freeman, Patrick Spenner, and Anna Bird of the Corporate Executive Board (CEB).

In their post, the authors wrote that shared values, not interactions, build loyal customer relationships. They defined shared value as "a belief that both the brand and customer have about a brand's higher purpose or broad philosophy" and cited a CEB study of 7,000 customers in the United States, the United Kingdom, and Australia showing shared value as "far and away the largest driver" in a brand relationship.

"To build relationships, start by clearly communicating your brand's philosophy or higher purpose," wrote the authors. While I don't agree entirely with their definitions of engagement and interaction, their insights about the significance of shared value is spot on.

Have We Reached the Summit?

Customer loyalty is genuinely important, but it is not the pinnacle or the endpoint. In a transparent world in which everyone can share their opinion, preference, joy, or anger *instantaneously with everyone else,* brands need more than loyal customers—brands need advocates!

Advocacy is incredibly, enormously valuable. Advocates not only spread the good word about your brand, they do your marketing for you! Ascending from loyalty to advocacy means more than simply moving up another level on the pyramid. It means you have crossed the frontier that separates traditional marketing from reverse marketing.

The Realm of Reverse Marketing

In the realm of traditional marketing, the brand does all the heavy lifting. When you enter the zone of reverse marketing, your customers share some of the load. They become evangelists and they actually do your marketing for you—by word of mouth and through social media. Customers can be wonderfully helpful if they love your brand, or dangerously destructive if they find a reason to hate your brand.

We haven't reached the highest level of the pyramid yet. At the top is co-creation. At the co-creation level, your customers not only love, buy, and actively promote your products—they help you improve your products so even more people will buy them.

Co-creation also applies to your messaging and content. When I got started in the communication industry, brands created content and distributed it to audiences. It was a one-way street. Brands pushed content and audiences consumed it.

There are very few places on earth where that model still works. Some brands haven't quite accepted that reality, but most brands understand that content is now a dialogue, not a monologue.

Smart brands want their customers collaborating and working alongside them to create content. The "brand of tomorrow" will focus less on creating its own content, and focus more on creating platforms that its customers will use to create and share content that drives conversations about the brand. We can look to Xiaomi (pronounced SHOW-me) as an example of this "brand of tomorrow," with which users are constantly driving the product development of this smartphone manufacturer. In just four short years, this user-centric company leaped to the number two position worldwide in the smartphone category. Xiaomi may be the forerunner of a new business model that is driven largely by user participation.

When your customers are helping you create the message (or even the product), it's not only more real and more honest—it's more effective.

Here's a question I'm hearing more often from clients: "What's the best way to keep our content aligned with the interests of our customer?"

My answer is usually a variation on this theme: When you enable your audience to co-create your content, the audience and the content will be naturally aligned.

It's Not a Race—It's a Dance

Traditional brand models assumed a lack of synchronization between a brand and its market. One would always be ahead, and the other would always be struggling to catch up. In a perfect world, however, brands and their markets would be so closely aligned that they would evolve together, changing and adapting continuously. This idea isn't as far-fetched as it seems. With machine learning, automation, and closed-loop decision systems, co-evolution could become a practical reality (see Figure 7.2).

Figure 7.2   The Idealized Brand Strategy Pyramid Would Include a Level of Continuous Co-Evolution

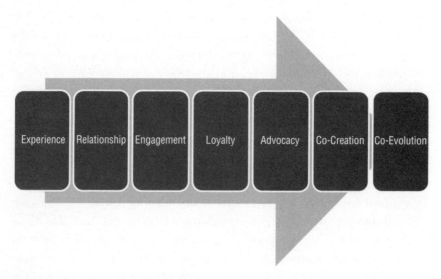

Figure 7.3   The Brand Strategy Pyramid Visualized as a Road Map of Logical Steps

Ideally, a brand and its audience would be like Fred Astaire and Ginger Rogers—always in motion, gliding through space and time with effortless grace, the dancers becoming indistinguishable from the dance.

The pyramid can also be visualized as a road map (see Figure 7.3), with a sequence of steps. Presumably, there would be a submenu of tasks for each step and a process for ensuring that steps aren't missed.

Don't Forget about IT

As mentioned earlier, everything depends on the customer experience. Remember, you have only one chance to make a good first impression. Today, most customers are likely to experience your brand for the first time on their smartphones or tablets. That means you not only need apps that look great and work flawlessly—you need seamless back-end integration with your IT department to ensure that you make good on whatever promises you're making to your customers.

There's a reason why Amazon is so popular—you push a button and a package containing the item you ordered arrives on your doorstep, usually within one or two days. Jeff Bezos invested huge amounts of time and capital in back-end systems designed specifically to support the customer interface that we call Amazon. In fact, Amazon's back-end IT systems are so good that Amazon "rents" them as cloud services to other businesses, including many startups that can't afford to build their own systems. Amazon Web Services is a whole other interesting story, but suffice it to say that Amazon is the poster child for successful front-end/back-end IT integration.

All of this is a long way of saying that in today's digital marketplaces, successful brand strategies require close working relationships with IT. Much has been written lately about the emergence of "shadow IT," which is what happens when a business unit or functional area of a company circumvents its CIO department and buys an IT service directly from a vendor or supplier.

The advantage of "shadow IT" is that it often enables smaller groups or teams within a company to move ahead rapidly on projects and campaigns. The downside is that without the pricing power and experience of the IT department, many of those semi-independent projects wind up costing more money than they would if the technology were acquired through normal channels. Additionally, when unexpected technical problems arise, the IT department is expected to jump in and resolve them—even though IT had no say in acquiring the products or services. As you might expect, those kinds of situations can create ill will and bad feelings that last for years.

My advice is simple and direct: Work with the CIO and the IT department as closely as you can. Make sure your web pages and your apps are functioning flawlessly and perfectly, every moment of every day. Don't give your customers a reason to defect to a competitor. Don't give your customers a reason to doubt your sincerity and your ability to keep your promises. Make sure everyone's primary experience with your brand is positive.

Remember, experience is the foundational level of the pyramid. All the higher levels are built on the assumption that you are providing positive experiences consistently. Many, if not most, of those experiences will take place on digital interfaces. It's your responsibility to make sure those digital interfaces are creating happy experiences for your customers. Your website and your mobile apps are windows into the soul of your brand.

It Isn't Easy Being Transparent

Let's face it, transparency isn't easy. Imagine you're the legendary Lady Godiva riding naked through town—except you have to do it every minute of every day, forever. Back in the good old days before the Internet and broadband networks, brands could hide their mistakes by keeping silent. Silence is no longer a practical strategy. In fact, your silence will only make it easier for your opponents and competitors to make you look bad.

One of my favorite authors, Nassim Nicholas Taleb, has coined a new term for the kind of strategies required in today's incredibly turbulent markets. In his 2012 book, *Antifragile: Things That Gain from Disorder,* Taleb makes the case for adopting a mindset that accepts the inevitability of chaos and disorder, and then figures out how to use them creatively to build value. It's sort of the ultimate version of taking lemons and turning them into lemonade.

In his book, Taleb asks us to imagine three categories of systems: fragile, robust, and antifragile. A fragile system breaks easily. A robust system can withstand more punishment, but eventually breaks. An anti-fragile system, however, doesn't buckle under pressure—it actually gets stronger! All the qualities that we usually imagine as bad (stress, disorder, chaos, mistakes, confusion, and so forth) are like snack food to an anti-fragile system. Instead of running away from danger and risk, an antifragile system embraces them.

"Embraces" is probably too strong a word. Let's just say that an an-tifragile system doesn't try to hide from the harsh realities of the world; it seeks to understand them and turn them to its advantage. Life itself, as Taleb notes, is antifragile. When ecosystems change and new pressures arise, species adapt and become stronger—or they become extinct.

KEY INSIGHTS

- Co-creation and collaboration are essential for successful reputation strategies.
- Reputation strategies and processes should be flexible, agile, and adaptable to endure continually changing business environments in turbulent markets.
- Brands can be built upon close customer relationship interaction.
- Customers can be your best sales team, and want to be.
- Reputation Strategy will depend on a close cooperation between marketing and IT to strategize and develop unique always-on benefits for the customer.

Note

1. Karen Freeman, Patrick Spenner, and Anna Bird, "Three Myths about What Customers Want," *Harvard Business Review,* May 23, 2012, http://blogs.hbr .org/2012/05/three-myths-about-customer-eng.

Chapter Eight

The Data Safety Net: Leveraging Evidence in the Midst of Crisis

Executive Summary: Understanding the layers within the communications ecosystem is essential for Reputation Strategy. Without granular and highly detailed knowledge, it's virtually impossible to respond quickly and effectively. Dynamic engagement requires multiple capabilities, including pattern recognition, digital listening, and analysis of signals that might indicate pending issues. The ability to collect and interpret evidence of impact is the new gold standard for the communications professional.

R emember the old movies in which people in powdered wigs and fancy costumes danced the minuet under crystal chandeliers in grand ballrooms? Those formal affairs were highly stylized rituals in which practically every step, gesture, and nuance was preordained and rigidly choreographed.

Sometimes it feels as though the older styles of corporate communications and public relations had a lot in common with those minuets. For the most part, communications processes were linear and mechanical, with little room for genuine improvisation. Tactical choices were limited, and results depended heavily on luck.

Today's version of communications resembles a mosh pit more than a minuet. Complexity reigns. There are no easy answers or surefire solutions. The old approach was like classical music; the new approach is more like jazz or hip-hop. You're continually improvising, monitoring responses, and tweaking the message for maximum effectiveness.

It used to be that the typical communications professional had a somewhat limited range of options when responding to a crisis or an event. Companies were really at the mercy of the media. When something happened, you could hold a press conference or issue a press release. Then you'd just cross your fingers and hope it worked. There weren't a lot of opportunities for following up.

Nowadays, the best communications professionals have access to data that enables them to understand who's really talking about the issue, who's sharing the information, who's picking up on the information that's been shared, which messages are resonating, and which messages are being incorporated into what people are actually writing about or sharing. The ability to collect, analyze, and understand data enables you to adjust and optimize your efforts much more effectively than ever before. (See Figure 8.1.)

For example, before the advent of digital media, it was common practice to issue a statement or a press release to the wires (for example, AP, UPI, Reuters) and then wait several weeks for a clipping service to send you physical clips from the newspapers and periodicals that had picked up or mentioned your release.

If you were incredibly lucky, a newspaper might actually assign a reporter to write a story about your release, and the reporter might call you on the phone to gather additional information. If the reporter was unusually nice, he or she might send you a copy of the article after it was published. Usually, though, you would have to wait for the clipping service to send you a clip of the article. At that point, several weeks

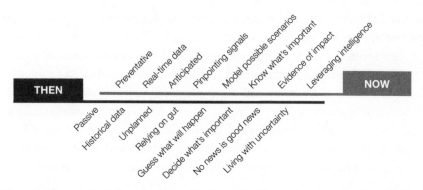

Figure 8.1   Crisis Then and Now: From Inevitable to Preventable

after speaking to the reporter, you would find out whether the article was favorable or unfavorable. If the article contained severe distortions, factual errors, or misrepresentations, you might contact the reporter and ask him or her to consider writing a more balanced follow-up article. Or you might contact another reporter at a different publication and pitch the idea of a follow-up article.

Most likely, however, you would let sleeping dogs lie, hope the storm would pass quickly, and wait for the next crisis to emerge.

Digital monitoring, predictive analytics, and a wealth of publishing platforms enable you to choose an approach that is more proactive and probably more effective. Today, we can do a much better job of understanding and in some cases predicting the life cycle of a crisis. Using next-generation data science, analytics, and digital monitoring, we better understand how information is moving across multiple platforms. Today, we have the ability to track how consumers are using and engaging with content. We have techniques to monitor which messages are getting traction and how information is being shared. We have a much more granular and more accurate perspective on what's really happening, and we can often observe the conversation evolving in nearly real time.

The ability to "see" how conversations evolve and migrate across digital platforms and social networks gives the communications professional a far wider range of options than ever before. We can see if a press release or statement is actually being picked up. If it's not being picked up, we'll know fairly quickly and we can decide whether we need a different approach.

In some instances, a story that hits the newswires at 9 A.M. might be "dead" by the following day. Or it might "have legs" and continue gathering attention for days. In the past, you could only guess. Now we have techniques and technologies that enable us to predict with greater accuracy whether an event will stay in the headlines or simply fade away.

In the past, the severity of a crisis would keep it in the headlines and the savvy professional would know instinctively what would be more than a one-day story. However, today, backed with more real-time data, what was once a gut check is now backed by evidence.

Word of Mouth versus Digital Listening

In many situations, the difference between what you *believe* is being said about your product or your company is very different from what is actually being said. In the past, we had to rely on word of mouth to shape our perceptions of the audience. Today, we can "listen" to digital conversations and get a much sharper picture of how an audience is responding.

Earlier in the book, I mentioned a case in which the client was absolutely convinced that its audience would react with extreme negativity to a pending product recall. The client instructed our team to prepare full-page newspaper advertisements apologizing for the recall. With great difficulty, the client agreed to wait until our team had completed a quick scan to determine what people were really saying about the client and its product. As it turned out, only a small handful of people were focused on the issue, and their conversations were limited in scope.

When we presented our evidence to the client, it became manifestly clear that the situation, though unfavorable, did not warrant a full-scale response. The data we gathered and analyzed indicated that the client's audience would take the news in stride, digest it, and move on.

Our ability to "listen" to the digital conversation—more or less as it was occurring—made a huge difference. Instead of going with a gut response that would have likely made the situation worse, the client took a step back and chose a better alternative.

It is important to understand that "digital listening" is about gathering data and studying it scientifically to look for signals that would give us a reasonably accurate idea of how an audience is likely to respond to a particular message or campaign. It's not a perfect science, but it's a significantly better way of dealing with problems than merely guessing.

When I think back on the early years of my career, I am certain that if we had access to even a fraction of what we have today in terms of new techniques and technologies for analyzing data, our decision-making process would have been much different. When you have access to data, you can step back and make genuinely better decisions.

Understanding When a Message Resonates

Another major difference between traditional and modern communications is the ability to gauge when a message is resonating with an audience. Early in my career, it was all about developing message points and then promoting them. Ideally, you would do opinion research and run focus groups to find out if your messages were likely to work. But when a crisis hits or some unexpected event occurs, you typically do not have time for that kind of research. In a crisis, organizations need real-time feedback from the people affected by the crisis.

Today, most companies and organizations have highly diverse audiences, spread across multiple countries and regions of the world. As a result, a message that resonates with one part of your audience might not resonate with another part of your audience. It's absolutely critical to have the skills and capabilities necessary to create different messages for different segments of your audience.

At the risk of sounding repetitive, there is no "one size fits all" solution. Complexity is the name of the game. Succeeding requires us to accept the fact that the twenty-first-century communications ecosystem is incredibly complicated and that modern reputational problems resist easy solutions.

Don't assume that no news is good news. If nobody responds to your statements or messages, it probably means your audience doesn't understand what you are trying to convey. In the past, if we didn't hear anything back from the audience, we assumed the story had run its course and that was the end of it. But you can no longer make those kinds of simplistic assumptions. Stories that seem dead can be very much alive in some corner of the digital ecosystem. That's why you need to keep listening.

When you're actively listening, you're much more likely to pick up on which messages are effective. You are also more likely to notice the warning signs when some part of your campaign is misfiring or heading in the wrong direction.

In addition to helping you understand which messages are working with the audience, digital listening provides you with tangible evidence of impact. In other words, you know who picked it up, how it's being shared, and who's talking or writing about it. Without that kind of specific knowledge, it's very difficult to manage a campaign effectively.

Evidence of impact is the new gold standard for the communications professional. That said, you need to know what kinds of evidence and which signals are truly meaningful. Just because you have the ability to gather and analyze data doesn't mean you have a substitute for strategy. You still need people with skills and experience to interpret the information and make decisions.

It's great to be monitoring three dozen signals, but which of those signals are really indications of a pending issue or problem? Which are triggers of a looming disaster? Which can you safely ignore, and which require your immediate attention?

The ability to perceive many different kinds of signals is less important than the ability to know which two or three of those signals actually matter. That's why it's unlikely that Reputation Strategy will become fully automated anytime in the near future—human judgment still plays a critical role in the process and we don't have an app for that.

KEY INSIGHTS

- Reputational events have a predictable life cycle.
- Conversations about brands often move across multiple digital platforms.
- Real-time monitoring helps brands identify and influence trends that can affect reputation.
- When dealing with a crisis, hard facts and clear evidence are essential for making good decisions.

- "Listening" across all platforms lets you witness what is being said and take immediate action, reinforcing and addressing what people want to hear and eliminating what is falling flat.
- Data on what is being said and where it's being said still requires intelligent human decision making in assessing next steps. In other words, while it is a necessary and critical resource, the data can't do it all.

Chapter Nine

Reputational Partnering

Executive Summary: Reputation depends on a complex blend of activities and relationships with external parties. One of the best ways to leverage an existing brand reputation (or to rebuild a damaged brand reputation) is through carefully structured partnerships. Having a robust system with clear rules and objective metrics is essential for ensuring partnerships deliver real value for all parties involved.

I n this chapter, we're going to look at the value of partnerships in campaigns and strategies designed to enhance or rebuild corporate brand reputation. As noted previously, we live in a social world. To phrase it more accurately, we live in a world of digitally interconnected multiple social ecosystems. The idea of going it alone when it comes to something as important as your brand's reputational strategy strikes me as strangely old-fashioned. From our perspective, the likely upside of partnering far outweighs the potential downside.

While the advantages and benefits of partnering seem obvious, what's not obvious is the level of effort, planning, and hands-on management required to make partnerships work for all parties involved. This chapter dives into the details of reputational partnering, and offers an in-depth look at a company that makes the most of its partnerships. For the purpose of our narrative, let's just say that it is a large multinational company that's been operating successfully in the customer products space for more than 100 years. Our source for this chapter is "Linda," a senior executive at the company.

Developing an Objective Process

In her role, Linda oversees a team that works closely with multiple business units of the company on a variety of broad-scale initiatives and strategic partnerships created to reflect and enhance the company's long-standing reputation and commitment to corporate citizenship.

She sat down with us recently and shared details of the innovative strategy the company has developed to leverage its reputation on a global stage. "We didn't just simply decide to do this. We have a 100-year tradition of corporate citizenship and making a positive social impact," Linda says. "It took a blend of research and practical experience to create an objective process that works effectively across a diverse company."

The drive toward creating an enterprise-wide process began in earnest during the global financial crisis of 2008–2009, when it became apparent the company's many philanthropic efforts—which significantly helped millions of people across the world—also represented a substantive corporate asset.

"As a company, we weren't promoting the wonderful philanthropic work we do. Other than a brief mention in our annual report, we weren't really talking about it," Linda says. But in the aftermath of the financial crisis, "the importance of social responsibility and company reputation began moving to the forefront. And if our philanthropic work is important, we should be talking about it."

The company's growing awareness of the reputational value of its philanthropy coincided with the rise of digital social marketing, which most traditional marketers had dismissed previously as a passing fad.

Digital social marketing created new opportunities for marketers who were ready to explore and who weren't afraid to challenge the status quo.

"We entered into the digital space through our philanthropic work. We entered it very strongly and as a result, we've been able to build our presence in a very important space," says Linda. "Digital social media is perceived as an authentic medium. It feels very real, which means that it's a great fit for us because our messages and our values are totally real and authentic."

Like many large firms, the company had separate organizations for corporate communications, marketing, and philanthropy. Today, those organizations work together under the umbrella of a global corporate affairs group, which is headed by a senior member of the company's management committee.

From my perspective, the company's approach seems both progressive and practical. The umbrella group bridges the gaps between the traditional silos, and creates an array of synergies that would have been impossible or impractical in the past. It helps that Linda's experience at the company includes posts in marketing and corporate communications. She understands the differences between the historical functions and is sensitive to the traditional rivalries. "I've lived on both sides, which makes it slightly easier for me to manage potential issues that might naturally arise," says Linda. "Everyone is passionate about their work, and that's natural. At the same time, people are moving beyond the traditional silos and learning how to collaborate across boundaries to achieve a broader strategic objective. It's really about sharing a sense of purpose."

That said, integrating the functions of three traditionally separate organizations is not a piece of cake. "It's like air traffic control," says Linda. "There are many important tasks requiring constant attention."

Partnerships Are Essential

Partnerships with a wide range of organizations and agencies are essential to the company's overall strategy of blending philanthropy, corporate communications, and marketing into a coherent strategy that generates tangible benefits for the company and the world around it.

As a general rule, partnerships that generate benefits for all parties involved do not spring into existence overnight. They must be carefully considered, nurtured, and managed over time. Indeed, one of the lessons Linda's team learned is that continual monitoring, measurement, and evaluation are absolutely fundamental to the success of the partnerships. There is, as Linda observes, no magical formula. It takes a mixture of research, practical experience, and serendipity to create and sustain viable partnerships.

Choosing the right partners isn't easy. Linda's team looks at three primary criteria—societal impact, operational impact, and reputational impact—when evaluating potential partners. "First, we want the partnership to have a positive impact on society. Second, it makes sense to leverage our partnership across our family of companies. Third, we want the partnership to elevate our reputation and the reputation of our partners. Ideally, both brands will gain from the partnership," Linda says.

A fourth consideration is size. Prospective partners need the scale and depth necessary to meet their obligations and hold up their end of the bargain. "You have to manage your partnerships with the same care that you manage other important parts of the business. You need good people, good contracts, good systems, and good oversight. It involves lots of work and dealing with many tough issues," Linda says. "At the end of the day, it's a business process."

Her team of consultants helped the company build a "partnership" model to monitor and measure the viability and trajectory of ongoing partnerships. "The model enables us to judge in quantifiable terms whether a partnership is working or not," says Linda. "We look at the four metrics (social, operational, reputational, and size) to help us make sure that partnerships are properly aligned and moving in the right direction."

The model enables Linda's team to manage a portfolio of partnerships with a set of objective criteria, similar to the way that an investor would manage a portfolio of equities. "In addition to showing us what's working and what's not working, it also reveals strengths, weaknesses, and opportunities that might be hard to see without an objective methodology," Linda says.

Employee Engagement

From my perspective, the company's systematic approach, with its methodologies and processes, is a far cry from the generally haphazard efforts I see at many other large corporations. The extra effort isn't just for show—it generates real value for the company.

Let's return to the idea of employee engagement, which falls under the category of operational impact in the partnership model. The company Linda works for is a highly decentralized modern enterprise. Decentralization offers benefits and poses challenges. One clear benefit of decentralization is agility—decentralized corporations can usually react more swiftly to changing market conditions than highly centralized corporations. One clear drawback to decentralization is that it sometimes makes it hard to inspire a genuine sense of enterprise-wide solidarity and shared purpose.

The operational impact metric in the partnership model can be viewed as a proxy measure of employee engagement. In other words, it takes employee engagement to ensure that partnerships work smoothly across the enterprise. Success tends to breed more success. As more employees become engaged, word spreads across the enterprise and more business units get involved. Like a rolling snowball—or an avalanche, depending on your perspective—good partnerships begin to gather and sustain their own momentum.

That's exactly what you want from a partnership—the sense that it is viable and self-sustaining. What you don't want from a partnership is the constant worry that it will falter or wind down after the initial excitement wears off.

Generating Value for All Parties

Sometimes there's a tendency to assume that a partnership based on shared values will automatically generate tangible value for the partners. That's a dangerous assumption and it can lead to the failure of the partnership, despite the best intentions.

It's critical to remember that all partnerships are based on deals between two or more parties. The deals must be perceived as fair by all of the parties involved. A partnership must generate some kind of tangible, measurable benefits for everyone involved. If it doesn't, the partnership won't deliver the returns that people are expecting, and it probably won't last.

When you're a large corporation with a strong brand, it's easy to overlook the fact that your partners—who are often smaller and less well-known—have their own needs, their own set of stakeholders, and their own expectations. That's why many of the reputational partnerships between large companies and small organizations break up— sometimes the larger brands just assume that they're doing the smaller brand a favor by partnering with them. My advice is to approach potential partnerships with the same caution and respect with which you would approach any important relationship. Do your due diligence and take the time to articulate clearly what all parties actually expect from the partnership and what they're capable of delivering.

After the partnership is formed, you need to monitor it carefully. Linda's team keeps a close watch on their partnerships. Maintaining a watchful posture is both labor intensive and time consuming, but absolutely necessary. "You need to keep feeding data to the data scientists," Linda says. "Collecting the data isn't easy, and it takes a lot of time, but you have to do it, or you're flying blind."

We've only skimmed the surface of the company's efforts, which are truly epic in scope. The company has pioneered the discipline of reputational partnering, and I'm delighted we had an opportunity to work with them in an area that's becoming increasingly fundamental to people and corporations all over the world.

KEY INSIGHTS

- Smart companies form partnerships to enhance their reputation.
- Digital communication technologies can and should be used for social good, creating value across broader audiences.
- Reputational partners must be carefully selected, and partnerships need to be managed for maximum effectiveness.

- Partnerships have to have more than shared values—there needs to be a win-win relationship.
- Clear goals and objective metrics are essential to ensuring an adequate Return on Partnership.
- In addition to providing external benefits, partnerships can also drive higher levels of employee engagement within your organization.
- Customers are used to a connected world, so partnerships are second nature to them at this point, and almost expected. It is, after all, a sharing economy.

Chapter Ten

The Reputation Culture

Executive Summary: Easy access to information about product quality is shifting the balance of power in favor of customers. But that doesn't mean brands are fighting an uphill battle. Information is a double-edged sword; it can be used by buyers and by sellers to achieve their objectives. The only certainty is that the reputation of a brand is shaped by information. Since customers form opinions about brands based on information generated by other customers, it makes sense for brands to develop capabilities for monitoring and analyzing relevant information, and knowing how to respond when problems seem imminent.

Y ou've heard it before: It's not the product itself that matters, it's what people *say* about the product that really counts. That's an exaggeration, of course, but there's always more than a grain of truth in the observation that in today's economy, style often trumps substance.

The made to order example of that phenomenon, of course, is Apple. For the most part, the products created and marketed by Apple are not technologically superior to the products sold by its competitors. But almost everyone seems to agree that Apple products are much cooler. And that perception has driven Apple sales for decades.

The Apple story perfectly illustrates the power of reputation. Apple has built a reputation for creating innovation—and they've translated that reputation into a wildly successful business. I think it's fair to say that in today's global economy, Apple's reliance on reputation is not unique. In fact, I would argue that it's rapidly becoming the standard model for success in hyper-competitive markets.

People say that loyalty isn't what it used to be, but I think they're missing the big picture. Customers are often fickle about individual products within a company's portfolio, but customer markets seem more brand-conscious than ever before. It's okay with Apple if customers "defect" from their Apple laptops to Apple iPads. Does Apple really care that when people started buying iPhones in significant numbers, the market for iPods essentially tanked? As long as Apple customers stick with the Apple brand, Apple is happy.

Here's an analogy: Let's say that every Saturday night, you order a cup of chicken noodle soup at your favorite local diner. If you suddenly stop ordering the chicken noodle and order a cup of pea soup instead, do you think the owner of the diner would really care? As long as you keep showing up on Saturday night and ordering soup, the owner will be delighted. And of course, there's always the chance that when you sit down for soup, you'll stick around and order a big dinner, which would make the owner really happy!

Focus on the Customer Experience

Our dinner analogy also affords us the opportunity to look briefly at the importance of focusing on the value of the customer experience itself and the role the customer plays in shaping that experience. Communicating effectively requires a lot more than simply pushing out messages. It is important to understand where messages are landing and more important how customers are interacting with that content.

The best organizations do not simply release messages; they create content that is engaging and inspire the reader to take an action. Organizations also track the impact of their content and are constantly taking feedback from customers and making adjustments to communications strategies in real time. They actively seek to understand how audiences perceive their message and are measuring impact regularly.

As they go through that process of following the actual trajectory of a message, they make decisions based on the insights generated by information they collect and analyze. Armed with those insights, they can ask themselves, "Are these messages working? Are they having the intended effect? Do we need to repeat them? Do we need to change them?"

It's worth mentioning again that we're all living and working within a vibrant ecosystem of communications channels. It's no longer sufficient to choose the right channel for sending a message to your audience—you also have to choose the right form of messaging for that particular channel.

It's also critical to remember that while you, the brand, might perceive one channel as being preeminent over another channel, your audience might see things differently, depending on how they're interacting with your brand.

Your reputation is your website, your call center, your smartphone apps, your direct mail campaign. Your reputation is also your IT department, your marketing team, your PR team, and your vendor partners. All of them, together and separately, have an impact on your reputation as a brand.

User experience sits at the center of how customers are interacting with brands and forming opinions on reputation. In building brands in today's complex environment, organizations must focus on creating the best possible experience for users. The user experience must be consistent across all channels, whether online or offline. When observing the market, I see strong connections between user experience and brand success. Increasingly, I am observing that user experience can make or break a new product or service.

Back to the Future?

Author Joshua Klein explores the body of thought emerging around the concept of reputational value in his excellent book *Reputation Economics: Why Who You Know Is Worth More Than What You Have.* In the book,

Klein does a deep dive into the cultural mechanisms of reputation, and I found his insights extremely valuable. From Klein's perspective, "reputation economics" is not an entirely new idea. In some respects, it represents a return to the commercial trading systems that were commonly used before the Industrial Age. Those systems were based largely on trust. We can argue about whether preindustrial commerce was better or worse than today's forms of commercial engagement, but there's a simple truth we can agree upon: there were far fewer people engaged in trade back then than there are today, and that made it easier for people to keep track of who was trustworthy and who wasn't.

If we are indeed reverting back to some form of a reputation-based economy, there are cultural implications. In an age when reputations can be easily tracked, cash value is less important than reputational value.

Why is that an important concept to consider? I believe that people who focus exclusively on the cash value of products and services are out of step with the times. Cash was important when trust was low. I'm sure you've all seen the sign, "In God We Trust, All Others Pay Cash." The sign usually makes us smile because we recognize the truth underlying the words.

The easy availability of information that you can use for deciding whether to trust or not trust someone means that cash no longer needs to be the sole substitute for trust. Instead, reputation is becoming the fallback substitute for trust. It's too early to say for certain that reputation will replace cash, but, for some, the signs of change are already emerging.

Until fairly recently, only major financial organizations had ready access to customer credit histories. If you've ever bought anything on credit, you know that's no longer the case. Your information is out there, floating around in the cloud. Tools for aggregating your information and instantly gauging your level of trustworthiness are easily available to anyone willing to pay for them. You don't need to be a big business anymore to have access to detailed information and practical analytic tools for making quick decisions about whether or not to trust someone.

"Tools now exist to take all of the billions of bits of information that you're generating every second and translate it all into accurate estimations about your behavior, your desires, and likely actions. . . . It's the ultimate instance of your reputation preceding you," Klein writes.

The same is true for corporations and organizations. They are empowered by what they learn about you and your products. In the past, customer complaints would often be ignored or dismissed. Today, customers don't hesitate to share their complaints with millions of fellow customers through social networks.

Thanks largely to the Internet, customers have power and they aren't afraid to exercise it. For most brands, the only viable defense is continuous monitoring of the digital ecosystem, followed by swift action.

Here's where many brands fall flat. Even when they detect the signals of a looming problem, they aren't sure of what to do next. Instead of following the evidence and digging deeper to discover what's really happening, they fall back on instinctive responses like denial or evasion. In some cases, they over-apologize or they apologize in a way that inadvertently makes a bad situation worse.

The natural urge to respond quickly is understandable, but it's also dangerous. Problems usually don't arise overnight and there are usually detectable early warning signs that create a window of opportunity to design the appropriate response. Even when the clock is ticking, you should take the time to consider your options. After reviewing your options, take another deep breath and test them to see which one is most likely to prove effective.

Controlled tests are the absolutely best way of figuring out in advance whether a campaign or tactic is likely to work. The CEO of a major gaming company often said there was only one way to get fired immediately from the company: *Don't use a control group.* I don't know whether he was kidding or not, but he made his point.

A/B Testing and Randomized Controlled Trials

One of Klein's observations focuses on the value of A/B testing,[1] which supports my belief that a scientific approach to Reputation Strategy is foundational to success. Although A/B testing and randomized controlled trials have been considered the gold standards in science for more than a century, marketers and communications professionals have been slow to pick up on their value.

My hunch is that over the next couple of years, the ability to perform quick A/B tests of proposed campaigns will become a differentiating competitive advantage for many brands, and that brands that don't develop the capabilities for running A/B tests will find themselves at a distinct disadvantage.

Five years from now, or possibly even sooner, the idea of launching any kind of campaign without initially running A/B tests will seem incredibly short-sighted. It seems reasonable to assume that A/B testing will become a best practice in the near future, and that it will be hard to win approval for a campaign or initiative that hasn't been scientifically tested.

You don't need to hire a brigade of data scientists to run A/B tests. Some of the best data analysis is done by small teams with fewer than eight people. What's really needed is a change in mindset, and the willingness to see that science is your ally, not your enemy.

Managing Change

Creating a culture of reputation within your organization is not an overnight project. It requires a strategy and a plan. Creating a culture of reputation means that everyone within an organization understands not only the importance of reputation on business success but is clear on how their roles directly affect reputation. I've often pondered the question of whether organizations need a chief reputation officer—someone who wakes up every morning thinking about what they are going to do to positively affect the reputation of a company. The truth is that it's not the job of one person to do this; everyone plays a critical role in building, managing, and defending reputations. Creating a culture of reputation means that there are systems, structures, and processes in place to reward and encourage decision making with reputation at the center of those decisions.

Creating change within organizations, especially established organizations, is very difficult. Much has been written about the importance of employee buy-in and instilling a sense of ownership across organizations as central to effective change.

Leadership and sponsorship are important, but proving the significance of context to employees and demonstrating the value of why change is necessary are equally important. Changing culture is a ground game and must permeate throughout entire organizations. While it is critical that there be effective engagement and communications from the most senior levels within an organization, true progress occurs at the grassroots level with front-line workers who, in many instances, are in positions of power every day to deliver on brand promises.

Although the term "change management" often seems a cliché, the processes of transforming an organizational culture are neither easy nor intuitive. Changing organizations is hard and there is often resistance, which is normal.

Another key lesson is that different people respond differently to change. You can't assume that everyone starts at the same place or moves at the same pace. "Leaders don't control change or uncertainty; they guide it, shape it, and influence it."

Consider the following primary disciplines when managing change within organizations.

1. **Stakeholder Analysis:** Having a clear understanding of the many groups affected by a change—and what exactly that impact will be. Mapping the "who and what" associated with the proposed change so that each group's unique values, culture, needs, and concerns can be addressed.

2. **Leading the Change:** Having clear sponsorship and governance, critical success factors for implementing change, and ensuring that change sponsors are supported by groups of people to lead the change effort. And, because not all good leaders are by default good change leaders, ensuring that they have the knowledge, skills, and abilities to be successful in this role is key.

3. **Change Strategy:** Having a clear plan for determining how to execute the change. A clear road map that identifies and defines phases of the change implementation from people, process, technology, and infrastructure contexts is key to driving and governing successful change. The road map should clearly define the activities, outputs, and outcomes associated with each phase of the change effort.

4. **Communicating the Change:** Engaging key stakeholders at all organizational levels—from C-level executives to frontline staff. Using well-planned and timely communication to ensure that every person affected thoroughly understands the change and the reason for it and has the opportunity to engage or provide feedback in the change effort.

5. **Human Capital Management:** Examining the flow of talent and skills within the organization to methodically address workforce plans affected by the change, development needs, and where new capabilities and restructuring are needed.

6. **Learning and Training:** Understanding not only what learning and training will be required for an implementation but also which components should be taught continually to inform the affected groups. Ongoing performance support is also key to sustaining the change and reaping the desired results.

7. **Business Process and Infrastructure:** Mapping current business processes to future ones will illuminate gaps. Needed process reengineering is a key enabler to successful change. This involves revisiting existing operating concepts and developing playbooks to enable the change.

8. **Project Management:** Understanding that project management methods, skills, and techniques are central to executing change and that a change manager must draw on project management to ensure clear decision rights, discipline, documentation, schedule management, issue resolution, knowledge sharing, and milestone management. This is about ensuring that change is achieved within the time, cost, and scope parameters of the initiative.

9. **Performance Management:** Applying a clear performance management approach, such as Balanced Scorecard, is key to the critical change management lever of reward and reinforcement. This is about amplifying pockets of success where the change is happening, and illuminating opportunities for continued improvement.

I deeply believe that developing and sustaining a genuine culture of reputation requires a comprehensive strategy for organizational change.

KEY INSIGHTS

- In many ways, Reputation Strategy is a return to principles that governed relationships between buyers and sellers in the past.
- In an age of nearly "perfect" information, sellers cannot rely on traditional marketing techniques to sway customers. They must think carefully about the customer experience.
- Customers value the opinions and beliefs of other customers, which is why reputation has become an increasingly critical differentiator and source of true competitive advantage.
- Developing a culture of reputation is not a short-term project that can be mandated from the top down. It must be approached with the same commitment, planning, and attention to detail required by a major business transformation project.

Note

1. A/B testing basically means comparing two versions of a web page, ad, or campaign and determining which version works better. There are a variety of ways to run A/B tests. The goal is removing doubt, guesswork, and bias from the decision-making process.

Chapter Eleven

The Reputation Payoff: The High Stakes of Crisis Leadership

Executive Summary: When a crisis strikes, people look to leaders for guidance and reassurance. Crisis leadership requires more than presenting a calm face; it requires understanding how humans function under extremely stressful conditions and knowing which leadership techniques will help people regain their composure and begin working together effectively to resolve the crisis.

I n Chapter 4, we discussed the value of positioning crisis management as a tactical capability within a larger framework of Reputation Strategy. In this chapter, I'd like to backtrack just a bit and take a deeper dive into the difference between crisis management and crisis leadership.

Today, organizations are expected to demonstrate competency in everything they do, including crisis management. No one will applaud you for merely remaining calm. When disaster strikes, people need more than reassurance—they need leadership. Increasingly, the ability to provide genuine leadership in a crisis is foundational to Reputation Strategy.

Eric McNulty has extensive experience exploring high-stakes crisis leadership. His official title is director of research and professional programs and program faculty at the National Preparedness Leadership Initiative (NPLI), a joint program of the Harvard School of Public Health and the Center for Public Leadership at Harvard's Kennedy School of Government. He's also an instructor at the Harvard School of Public Health.

Eric is the principal author of the NPLI's case studies on responses to the Boston Marathon bombing, Hurricane Sandy, and the *Deepwater Horizon* oil spill. He and his colleagues have also studied the response to the September 11 attacks and observed leaders in the midst of events from Hurricane Katrina to the N1H1 virus pandemic and the 2015 Ebola outbreak in West Africa. Eric spoke at length with our team about the relationship between crisis leadership and Reputation Strategy. We began by asking Eric to describe how good leaders prepare their organizations—and prepare the people in their organizations— to respond effectively when a crisis occurs. Here are Eric's replies, summarized and lightly edited.

The principles that allow you to lead through a crisis are essentially the same as your everyday leadership principles, except they're brought into high relief. If you practice good basic leadership every day, you'll be ready when the crisis happens.

The best leaders prepare ahead of time. They schedule drills and exercises. They measure and test how their teams respond under simulated conditions. They look for holes in their plans— remember, you want to find the flaws and fix them before the crisis, not during the crisis.

They make crisis response planning into a team activity. They schedule brown-bag lunches with their teams to talk about "what keeps you awake at night." You'd be amazed how helpful it is when your team sits down together and talks about handling a potential crisis. Just discussing it helps prepare you emotionally for the day when it actually happens, because you feel as though you've already got some experience—even if the experience was only a conversation over lunch.

Some of the companies we work with do table-top exercises to test their processes and protocols. The exercises usually last two or three hours, and they really help people to see the various aspects of the response plan. When they're done well, those exercises can even simulate the emotional stress of a real crisis. The important part is getting people comfortable and preparing them in advance for a difficult experience.

During a crisis, it's natural to experience a range of emotions. As a crisis leader, being aware of your own emotions will help you deal more effectively with the emotions of the people around you.

The Crisis Never Reads Your Plan

We asked Eric to talk about specific lessons he and his team learned from crises such as Hurricane Katrina, the *Deepwater Horizon* oil spill, and the Boston Marathon bombing.

Of all the lessons we learned, one stands out clearly: The crisis never reads your response plan. No matter how carefully you plan, the crisis will challenge you. So you must be agile and flexible, because you'll need to adjust your plan in the midst of a highly stressful situation.

In other words, you cannot simply count on sticking to your plan and checking off the boxes on your checklists—because the crisis hasn't read your plan and it doesn't care about your checklists. If the crisis followed your plan, it wouldn't be a crisis—it would just be a problem and you would manage it.

Hurricane Katrina, unfortunately, was a great example of that. My colleague Dr. Lenny Marcus was on the scene and observed that the folks at FEMA (Federal Emergency Management Agency) were ready for a hurricane. They knew how to respond to hurricanes, which are wind events. But when the levees broke in New Orleans, Katrina became a flood, which is a water event.

The people in charge had a really hard time shifting their mindset and accepting the idea that a wind event had become a water event. That's when Katrina became a true crisis.

In the case of the *Deepwater Horizon* oil spill, the response plan was shaped largely by the Oil Pollution Act (OPA) of 1990, which was passed after the *Exxon Valdez* spill. The *Valdez* was a single vessel, containing a finite amount of oil. The *Deepwater* spill involved multiple commercial entities and an unknowable quantity of oil gushing from a leak roughly 5,000 feet below the water's surface.

OPA had worked fine for hundreds, even thousands, of smaller oil spills, but the magnitude and complexity of the *Deepwater* spill was unprecedented. On top of that, you had multiple government agencies with different constituencies and different approaches to solving problems.

One of the lessons we learned from the *Deepwater Horizon* spill is that when a crisis strikes, it's not unusual for conflicts to arise among the parties involved, at least initially. Some people will point fingers. Some people will begin looking for a "bad guy." Cooperation slows down and the crisis takes longer to resolve.

In a crisis, organizations that should be collaborating can shift into a conflict mode. Why does that happen? It happens because everyone is under stress. Different people make different assumptions. Crises tend to generate confusion, and that confusion can lead to conflict. You'll need to manage the conflict, bring people together, help them collaborate, and focus their energies on solving the crisis.

Eric said that the value of preparing and drilling for all aspects of a crisis became evident during the Boston Marathon bombing response. Many agencies were involved in the response, but they acted in concert to mitigate the crisis. The city's hospitals, which are normally quite competitive, worked together seamlessly throughout the crisis, thanks largely to years of training and preparation. After the crisis, doctors, nurses, and emergency responders from the hospitals sat down together to review the city's response and to share lessons they'd learned from the tragic events of the day.

We like to say there should be no secrets in safety, even among competitors. When the bombs went off, the entire city rallied together. When there's some kind of major event, everyone suffers. Getting people working together during a crisis is an absolutely critical part of leadership.

We've also found that the best leaders are intensely curious about their own roles and about the roles of the people around them. They're like ancient Kung Fu masters, always practicing and always trying to get better.

That curiosity and drive for self-improvement is connected to the reputation piece of crisis leadership. Great leaders know they can't outsource crisis leadership to PR teams or marketing specialists. Great leaders understand that it takes a long time to rebuild a damaged reputation. They also understand that when a crisis hits, you must respond effectively—because if you don't, you create a second crisis that can have a severe impact on your reputation.

Why is reputation so important? Part of the reason is due to a phenomenon called "confirmation bias." Essentially, confirmation bias means we tend to believe what we already believe. So when we believe that an organization is "good" (that is, it has a "good reputation"), we will continue believing that it is good until something happens that undermines our belief.

Organizations with good reputations get the benefit of the doubt. Organizations with less-than-stellar reputations are sometimes assumed to be guilty, even when they're not.

Rightly or wrongly, your reputation can depend on how well you handle a crisis. That's a prime motivation for preparing yourself and your team for a crisis—if you can't handle a crisis effectively when it occurs, your reputation will suffer.

Since it's hard to pin down the boundary between "crisis management" and "crisis leadership," we asked Eric to define the differences between the two in specific terms.

Management is more about the "what" and leadership is more about the "why." Management and leadership require different sets of complementary skills. They're both essential for getting through a crisis. But crisis leadership involves taking a much broader and longer view. Crisis leadership means looking at the full range of implications, across all of the stakeholders. In addition to solving the immediate problem, crisis leaders consider larger implications.

They tend to look at the crisis in terms of three time frames: immediate, intermediate, and long term. It's not just saying, "Let's get through this." It's thinking and considering, "How will this crisis affect us next year? How will it affect us five years from now?"

Dealing with the Psychology of Crisis

Crisis leadership also involves handling the psychological dimensions of a crisis. Human beings are emotional creatures. We've all heard executives say things like, "Let's keep our emotions out of this," "Let's just be rational," and "Let's just go with the facts." But in a crisis, many people find it extremely difficult to process information logically and behave rationally.

A good crisis leader engages with people on an emotional level— because at the beginning of a major crisis, the typical human response is emotional. When your brain senses a threat, it pushes everything else out of the way and focuses on basic survival. Daniel Goleman, the author of *Emotional Intelligence: Why It Can Matter More Than IQ,* calls it "the amygdala hijack," because the amygdala is the part of our brain that reacts to threats. Sometimes, as Goleman notes, the emotional response can be far greater than the actual threat. We asked Eric to talk about the best ways for leaders to reduce or ameliorate the natural urge to overreact in a crisis.

As a leader in a crisis, one of your first responsibilities is helping people move past their natural "freeze, flee, or fight" responses so they can begin processing complex information and behaving rationally. The crisis leader needs to understand what's happening to people on an emotional level and guide them back to a psychological space where they can do their jobs again.

When a crisis strikes, people tend to hunker down and withdraw or panic because of that amygdala hijack; they go into what our former NPLI colleague Dr. Isaac Ashkenazi calls "the emotional basement." Good crisis leaders help people "reset" their brains so they can manage their fears and resist the primitive messages from their amygdala. One of the best ways of accomplishing that is by focusing your teammates on simple tasks that you're sure they can do, no matter how upset they might seem. Ask them to restart their laptops, check their network connections or just count to 10 while taking deep breaths—doing any small task that demonstrates basic competence tends to calm people down and makes it easier for them to think rationally.

Dr. David Rock, the co-founder and director of the Neuro-Leadership Institute, has identified five social qualities that "enable employees and executives alike to minimize the threat response."[1] He uses the acronym SCARF, which stands for status, certainty, autonomy, relatedness, and fairness. We've found that David's model is extremely useful and definitely worth taking into consideration when you're formulating a crisis leadership strategy.

The SCARF model corresponds to basic human tendencies that cannot be safely ignored during a crisis. For example, brain research has shown that humans are hardwired to judge and appreciate the relative "fairness" of situations. As a result, people tend to accept solutions that appear fair, even when those solutions are less than optimal. Since almost every crisis involves choosing between several less-than-perfect options, good leaders will take the time to explain why they picked Option A over Option B or Option C, and why Option A represents the fairest choice.

It's also important to remember that not everyone will transition from panic mode to working mode at the same tempo. Some people on your team will require more time to adjust than others. As a leader, it's never safe to assume that everyone is on the same page. In fact, it's best to assume that people will adapt to the crisis at different speeds and in different ways. It's not enough for the crisis leader to be thinking rationally—the rest of the team also needs to be thinking and acting rationally.

People who have been through a similar crisis before will usually take less time to adapt than others. Use them to help reassure others just as a coach calls on players with playoff experience to help rookies gain focus. Since everyone will adjust at their own pace and in their own style, it's critical for the leader to show empathy and patience.

It's also important to remember that during a crisis, leadership can emerge from unlikely places. Here's a good anecdote that Eric shared.

> When I worked in the event management business, something would always go wrong, usually at the worst possible time. When something bad happened, one of our colleagues would always ask, "Is anyone bleeding from the head?" Of course, the answer was "no" yet somehow, hearing her say that always put the problem—whatever it was—in the proper perspective and made it easier for us to begin working on the right solution.
>
> Officially, she wasn't the boss. I was. But when something unexpected happened, her leadership qualities emerged and they were always appreciated. I learned from that experience that leadership isn't about your rank or your business title; it's about your behavior. Leadership can come from anywhere in your organization, and you need to recognize that, and be open to it when it emerges spontaneously. Sometimes, you will be led by the people who work for you—and that's okay.

Our conversation with Eric reminded us of the old-fashioned idea that true character is often revealed by crisis. In the same way that people are biologically hardwired to judge fairness, people also seem to have a natural ability to tell how well—or how poorly—other people respond to a crisis. Are they calm? Are they honest? Are they helpful? Are they effective? Are they moving forward and making progress? Are they resilient?

That's where the reputational risk lies. People expect bad things to happen occasionally, and they're often willing to forgive you for making mistakes. But they will be looking at you and your organization very closely during a crisis and they will be judging your response. Your reputation will hang in the balance. If people think you're handling the crisis well, your reputation will be enhanced. If they think you're doing a bad job, your reputation will be damaged. Undoing that damage can take years.

Great leaders prepare for success—and they prepare for failure. As humans, we tend to focus on success and downplay the chances of failure. We're all naturally optimistic, and that's perfectly fine. But as leaders, we also must be realists who understand that when a crisis occurs, we will be expected to be prepared to provide visible and effective leadership. There are plenty of executive responsibilities we can safely delegate to others, but crisis leadership isn't one of them.

The textbook example of the "right way" to deal with a crisis took place in October 1982, after someone replaced Tylenol Extra-Strength capsules with cyanide-laced capsules, resulting in the deaths of seven people. The Department of Defense wrote an excellent case study[2] about that horrific event, and it's worth reading today. Tylenol's maker, Johnson & Johnson, forthrightly acknowledged the severity of the event and moved swiftly to prevent a reoccurrence of the tragedy. One of my former colleagues took part in the crisis response, and I find his observations especially useful.

> When a crisis of that magnitude occurs, that's when your company's values, character, and reputation equity are really put to the test. Great companies recognize that they have a responsibility not only to address the immediate issue, but to demonstrate that they're taking corrective steps to ensure that whatever the problem is, it can't happen again.

In the wake of the Tylenol crisis, for example, Johnson & Johnson did more than just pull products from shelves—the company also changed the way Tylenol was packaged. In effect, J&J reengineered and redefined the concept of packaging to make it significantly less likely similar events would occur in the future. The changes in packaging were expensive, but necessary to address potential safety risks *and* to preserve the company's reputation.

In the years since the Tylenol tragedy, some people have wondered if J&J's response would have been different if it had been a business-to-business (B2B) enterprise and not a business-to-customer (B2C) enterprise. I believe that it would not have made a difference and that J&J would have responded the same way even if it had been a B2B enterprise. I also think that in today's digitally networked global markets, the distinction between B2B and B2C companies has become increasingly blurred.

Sooner or later, every company's products or services are used by people, and that makes every company a B2C enterprise, no matter what it calls itself.

More to the point, I believe that J&J's response was in large part determined by the essential character of the company. J&J's response didn't come out of nowhere—to a certain extent it was preordained. J&J did the right thing because it was—and still is—a company with strong core values and a deeply anchored sense of integrity. J&J began building its reputation in 1886, the year of its founding. When tragedy struck, J&J had the reputational equity it needed to weather the storm.

KEY INSIGHTS

- Every crisis creates a "flight or fight" response that must be recognized and managed.
- Crisis management is usually a zero sum game that deals with the crisis at hand, whereas crisis leadership creates win-win opportunities for the company and its stakeholders in the present and in the future.
- Great leaders—and great brands—don't just prepare for success; they also prepare for failure and they know how to respond effectively when a crisis occurs.
- Crisis management has to take into account that people respond differently to crisis. There has to be a plan that encompasses all reactions.

Notes

1. David Rock, "Managing with the Brain in Mind," *Psychology Today* 56 (Autumn 2009), www.psychologytoday.com/files/attachments/31881/managingwbrain-inmind.pdf.
2. "Case Study: The Johnson & Johnson Tylenol Crisis," U.S. Department of Defense, Crisis Communication Strategies, www.ou.edu/deptcomm/dodjcc/groups/02C2/Johnson%amp;20&%20Johnson.htm.

Chapter Twelve

The Future of
Reputation Strategy

D igital media has democratized the field of communications, toppling or unraveling the traditional hierarchies and disrupting the status quo. Today, most of us are connected through multiple social platforms and networks, nimbly living in an "always on" reality in which we can digitally buy, share, create, connect, and consume content in so many ways that it opens up a vast and exciting universe.

This always-on life has been 20 years in the making, first described circa 1998 as "A system that is online and ready to go 24 hours a day. Nothing has to be turned on or dialed up in order to use it. DSL and cable modems are examples of always-on technologies. . . ." Mobile technology is credited with propelling customer adoption of an always-on lifestyle in a relatively short period of time.

No wonder organizations have barely had a chance to catch up. This brave new digital universe holds up the perils for those who resist and those who are unprepared, leaving many committed organizations lagging way behind in their participating in the always-on reality with their users. Many organizations are wrestling with their mobile, data driven transformation and forecasts are hazy and unclear. Companies struggle to get the data they need activated at the right time in the right way. They find it challenging to use data effectively and collaboratively. There are also obstacles to generating trustworthy big data upon which businesses rest.

In this book, we've envisioned a future in which long-term relationships matter more than short-term transactions, and reputation becomes a more tangible yardstick by which we can measure brand equity. The scenarios and events recounted in this book support the view that reputation reflects an always-on viewpoint, with clear metrics and economic value.

As an asset, its value can grow or decline, depending on a variety of factors. Taken further, I think it's fair to say that reputation has become a form of economic exchange. You can't spend it at the supermarket, but it has economic power. I don't think it's unreasonable to suggest that most people view reputation as a price signal. In other words, companies with great reputations can charge higher prices than companies with poor reputations. Therefore, the overarching takeaway I've put forward is that reputation is an asset that can provide direct evidence of a brand's market vitality. As a result, the task of growing an organization's reputation will increasingly become a function of the C-Suite and corporate boardrooms. To lead, they will need a new generation of real-time data analytics to plot a seemingly and dynamically effective strategy. My work has shown that reputation can be monitored, measured, and managed over time for maximum return on investment. From my standpoint, investing in reputation makes good business sense.

On a broader stage, companies with great reputations can focus tier marketing resources on building profitable long-term relationships with high-value customers instead of engaging in relentless price wars that ultimately strip profits from the bottom line. When organizations focus on building up their reputation, they can worry less about vacuuming up leads for their sales funnels and pay more attention to meeting the real needs of their customers and communities. I truly believe that when organizations focus on reputation, they broaden their appeal and greatly improve their opportunities for entering and succeeding in new markets.

My hunch is that the winners in tomorrow's markets will be the organizations that invest today in the data, processes, and technologies necessary for managing reputation as a long-term strategic asset within the context of a hyper-connected, eco-complex world.

In its simplest terms, succeeding in the always-on environment is a core component of optimizing reputation as an asset. It is driven by understanding how to gather and distribute data between functions and across platforms in a way that enhances customer interaction with your product.

In economic terms, data will propel the evolution of an always-on business model, because data is what animates core business strategies such as communications. The methodologies, systems, and technologies to create an organizational model that can respond to customers in this eco-complex environment will translate directly into higher revenue.

Generally speaking, this approach can be captured in three basic steps:

1. Centralize data science but decentralize data distribution. "Think globally, act locally" applies to data as well as environmentalism. We have the technologies to allow data to be centrally optimized and then adapted to flow to organizational points where it can be most effective.
2. Use data to develop a "closed-loop" culture. This requires organizations to reorient toward outcome-based campaigns that have clear deliverables.
3. Build new organizational models to support an always-on customer. New customer demands will expose gaps between user experience and organizational capacity to deliver in this newly connected world. This is where new revenue and growth lies.

As new technologies transform our world, they also transform the way we work and how businesses are organized. The use of technology creates the need for workflows that become the new normal for efficiency and effectiveness.

I recall delivering a dinner speech at the Global PR Summit in beautiful Miami, Florida. I was granted a coveted speaker slot at the end of a two-day summit in between cocktails by the pool area and the distribution of the widely anticipated 2014 Sabre Awards. At the time of the speech, I was just starting my journey of looking into the role that analytics was playing in Reputation Strategy.

Over the course of a 25-minute speech, I made the case for the use of data and insights derived from data to aid Reputation Strategy and also the creative process. I talked about the role that data integration plays in allowing executives the ability to make more sense of the data they have within their organizations. I waxed on about how important it was for progressive organizations to break down barriers within agencies and create business models and teams that integrated computer science expertise, technologists, and economists with journalists, creative directors, and PR professionals.

There are many new entrants to the field of communications and reputation strategy. A short five years ago, we would not have mentioned analytics in the same sentence as reputation. I firmly believe that we must embrace the uncertainties of the future. The road ahead will be difficult. Neither Siri nor Google Maps will aid us on this journey of change within the profession. I often challenge my colleagues by asking them, "Do you want to be the change or would you rather read about what others have done to change our industry"?

I've spent the last 11 chapters sharing examples of the ways the business of communications and Reputation Strategy is changing and has changed. Technology, mobility, and more importantly, our ability to gather, curate, mine, and analyze data has led to much of the disruption within our industry. Over the course of this book, I've presented the argument that, given that so much information is moving through some form of digital means, the way we understand and engage with audiences has changed forever. As an industry, we can now be more precise in our efforts to engage with audiences. Advances in computer science and next-generation analytics, when applied to media and communications, have fundamentally changed the way professionals practice public relations.

I was asked in a breakfast event recently if I felt the public relations field was a dying industry. Had you asked me that question a few years ago, I would have paused and not had an answer. However, my answer was clear in this instance, "Absolutely not." I believe that as an industry, strategic communications is more needed now than ever before. There is broad recognition among chief executives of the power of reputation in government, private industries, and the nonprofit market sectors. And, while I believe in the role that technology will play in defining our industry, there is no computer, no computer program, nor an algorithm that can replace what professionals contribute every day: creativity, imagination, and experience. Yes, technology and analytics are important. Technology and analytics enable us to do our jobs better, faster, smarter, and with more precision. We are more confident about the decisions we make and counsel we provide as a result of the valuable insights and information we have access to in business.

What Next?

As I ponder the future of communications and Reputation Strategy, I'll offer the following predictions:

- **New and emerging reputation-based markets** will transform business, commerce, and society. Think about it. How many decisions are you making today without some consideration to reputation in the form of a review, ranking, word of mouth marketing, feedback, or experience tracker? Reputation is currency and will facilitate and enable more business transactions.
- **Digital and analytic functions** will no longer sit as stand-alone departments within consulting firms, agencies, or organizations. These functions are central to all business functions and Reputation Strategy in particular, and will be integrated into every facet of organizations.
- **Companies that embrace the true integration** of technology, marketing, and communications will lead in shaping the future of the industry. All others will be slow followers, and catching up will not be easy. True integration is not solely an exercise in organizational design or redesign. Business transformation will be about change management. Commit, learn along the way, be willing to fail, and move fast.
- **The communications and marketing organizations workforce of the future** will include behavioral economists, computer scientists, programmers, design thinkers, and technology experts. Marketing and IT will become co-dependent departments. This is

not to suggest that traditional liberal arts and communications degrees, like my undergraduate degree in philosophy, will be obsolete, but in order for companies to compete in tomorrow's always-on environment, new skill sets will be needed.

- **Content will be created by consumers** and we are all consumers. Progressive companies will partner with their customers on innovation, product development, and content creation. This takes nothing away from the role of the communications professional and reputation strategists. In fact, it will enhance their roles and place more emphasis on the role of the consumer in shaping reputation.

- **Listening will be more important than monitoring.** In his 2008 book *Words That Work,* Frank Luntz says, "It's not what you say but what they hear that's important." Truer words have never been spoken. With advances in digital listening, organizations will need to listen more to their customers than ever before. And listening will not be enough in the Reputation Strategy field. We will need to make connections to multiple conversations occurring in real time across the world in addition to connections to other relevant data. A truly massive undertaking in the past but one that is doable with the help of modern technology and next-generation advanced analytics.

Conclusion

We're still in the early decades of the twenty-first century but it is already clear that people are much more globally connected now than ever before, and there's no going back. For many consumers and organizations, reputation is a reflection of their character, whether good or bad. A good organization is more attractive at every level than a bad organization. From a business perspective, "good" usually translates into a competitive advantage resulting in higher revenue and fewer problems.

The stakes could not be higher for organizations that evolve to meet their users' insatiable need to be connected on their own terms. The rewards are unparalleled, but the reputational risks reflect real business risks. Through the lens of reputation, organizations can ask probing questions: Can your organization keep pace with the expectations of consumers? Is your organization's reputation helping or hurting sales? Does your reputation attract or repel potential partners? Would your organization be more effective or more profitable if it had a better reputation?

I had a conversation recently with a colleague in which we explored the role of the Internet. We pondered the question of what the Internet was really about. Is it about connecting people, sharing information, or helping facilitate commerce and trade? We came to the conclusion that while the Internet serves all of those functions and many more, the Internet was not invented to connect people; it was invented to facilitate the transfer of information. And while the Internet was a breakthrough and uncertain notion when it first came on the scene, today it has transformed every aspect of our lives.

Reputation and Reputation Strategy are at a similar inflection point. Reputation Strategy is not a new concept and few people will diminish its importance. However, reputation has always been an elusive phenomenon that was difficult to quantify. Consultants would often cringe at the question "How do we measure the impact of a Reputation Strategy?" And, while we've worked hard toward a common set of reputation metrics, we are on the verge of a new frontier of being able to use science and technology to quantify reputation, resulting in true business and economic value. We are experiencing explosive growth in the field of Reputation Strategy. And, whether or not you believe that technology or analytics will facilitate this transformation, one thing is clear: A change is happening that we cannot stop.

Recommended Reading

Christensen, Clayton M., and Michael E. Raynor. *The Innovator's Solution: Creating and Sustaining Successful Growth*. Boston: Harvard Business Review Press, 2003.

Cohen, Jared, and Eric Schmidt. *The New Digital Age: Transforming Nations, Businesses and Our Lives*. New York: First Vintage Books, 2014.

Collins, Jim. *Good to Great: Why Some Companies Make the Leap . . . and Others Don't*. New York: HarperCollins, 2001.

Cukler, Kenneth, and Viktor Mayer-Schönberger. *Big Data: A Revolution That Will Transform How We Live, Work, and Think*. Boston: Mariner Books, 2014.

Diamandis, Peter H., and Steven Kotler. *Abundance: The Future Is Better Than You Think*. New York: Free Press, 2012.

Duhigg, Charles. *The Power of Habit: Why We Do What We Do in Life and Business*. New York: Random House, 2012.

Dweck, Carol S. *Mindset: The New Psychology of Success*. New York: Random House, 2007.

Gladwell, Malcolm. *Outliers: The Story of Success*. New York: Little, Brown, 2008.

Kahneman, Daniel. *Thinking, Fast and Slow*. New York: Farrar, Straus and Giroux, 2011.

Klein, Joshua. *Reputation Economics: Why Who You Know Is Worth More Than What You Have*. New York: Palgrave Macmillan, 2013.

Kotter, John P. *Leading Change*. Boston: Harvard Business School Press, 1996.

Prahalad, C. K., and M. S. Krishnan. *The New Age of Innovation: Driving Co-created Value Through Global Networks*. New York: McGraw-Hill, 2008.

Ridley, Matt. *The Rational Optimist: How Prosperity Evolves.* New York: Harper Collins, 2010.

Simonson, Itamar, and Emanuel Rosen. *Absolute Value: What Really Influences Customers in the Age of (Nearly) Perfect Information.* New York: Harper Business, 2014.

Taleb, Nassim Nicholas. *Antifragile: Things That Gain from Disorder.* New York: Random House, 2012.

About the Book

Meet Our Experts

Erin Byrne is managing partner, chief engagement officer at Grey Healthcare Group. Byrne has more than 20 years of digital media experience spanning all areas of the online landscape. She is a sought-after counselor to C suite executives looking to navigate integrating digital and social media in the highly regulated and rapidly changing health care environment.

Byrne's diverse experience combines social media, digital technology, corporate communications, and integrated marketing with a specialty in social and mobile communications. She has experience across therapeutic areas and focuses on leveraging digital media to create more educated customers, enhancing the patient-to-physician relationship to create better health care experiences, and driving desired actions that meet business needs and create healthier outcomes. She also has strong expertise in developing social and digital media task forces, conducting organizational digital training, and helping companies govern their digital participation.

Byrne leads the digital media capability at the agency and is responsible for delivery of integrated digital strategy and execution to the agency's clients around the world. She is a member of the executive committee and sits on the global WPP digital advisory board. She also sits on the Text4Baby national steering committee that oversees Text4Baby, called the country's most success mobile health initiative, and is on the board of directors of InMed Partnerships for Children, an international humanitarian organization. Byrne is a frequent speaker on topics relating to digital media in health care, and contributes to the Dose of Digital health care blog.

Before joining the agency, Byrne created the digital media practice at Burson-Marsteller, where she worked for 12 years, most recently in the role of chief digital strategist.

Yasmin Crowther is chief of strategy and research at big data and digital intelligence firm Polecat. Polecat was founded in 2007 to provide advanced digital analytics and intelligence to many of the world's leading corporations and consultancies. Yasmin is also co-founder of sustainability strategy consultancy and think tank Shine.

She was previously head of consulting at SustainAbility, CSR director at international communications agency Ketchum, and strategic risk manager at environmental consultancy URS Dames & Moore. Her clients include many of the world's leading corporations and institutions. She is a published author and editor of numerous thought leadership publications, available at www.shinesustainability.com.

Martis "Marty" Davis is founder and president of the Applied Communications Institute, an organization dedicated to exploring new ways to use communications as a primary tool for individuals, organizations, and government entities to better affect public policy for a positive outcome. He has previously served as director of national media relations for AARP, where he led AARP's national media relations team's efforts for print, broadcast, and digital media.

Davis also has served as managing director of health care for Burson-Marsteller, where he was responsible for the development of marketing communications strategies and programs for many of the largest global pharmaceutical companies in support of their efforts to increase brand awareness, understanding, and usage of product offerings. He also drafted and managed legislative initiatives on behalf of national health insurers, fledgling pharmaceutical companies, and Internet startups in the health care field.

He served in the Clinton administration as Deputy Assistant Secretary for Public Affairs, Department of Health and Human Services during the administration's efforts to create and pass its version of health care reform. He has served as deputy commissioner of public affairs for the New York Health and Hospitals Corporation, the nation's largest municipal hospital system, and served on the Healthcare System Development Commission to improve the delivery of health care in the District of Columbia.

Patrick Ford is vice chairman and chief client officer at Burson-Marsteller. Before entering his current role, he served for six years as the firm's U.S. CEO. He also serves as chair of the firm's Asia–Pacific region.

He has advised a wide range of clients on corporate reputation management, senior executive positioning, media strategy, and crisis communications during a 25-year career at Burson-Marsteller.

Before joining Burson-Marsteller, he served as vice president for external affairs at the American Enterprise Institute for Public Policy Research in Washington, D.C.

He serves on the boards of trustees of the Institute for Public Relations and the LAGRANT Foundation. Ford is a member of the advisory board of the Scripps Howard School of Journalism at Hampton University.

Eric J. McNulty is director of research and professional programs and program faculty at the National Preparedness Leadership Initiative (NPLI), a joint program of the Harvard School of Public Health and the Center for Public Leadership at Harvard's Kennedy School of Government. He is a widely published business author, speaker, researcher, and thought leadership strategist.

McNulty writes a regular online column for Strategy + Business and is a contributing editor to Business Review (China) and the Center for Higher Ambition Leadership. He has written multiple articles for the *Harvard Business Review* (HBR) as well as articles for *Harvard Management Update, Strategy and Innovation, Marketwatch,* the *Boston Business Journal,* and *Worthwhile* magazine, among others. His HBR cases have been anthologized through the HBR paperback series and have been used in business education curricula in the United States and as far away as France and the Philippines.

He is the co-author, along with Dr. Leonard Marcus and Dr. Barry Dorn, of the second edition of *Renegotiating Health Care: Resolving Conflict to Build Collaboration* (Jossey-Bass, 2011). He is co-author of a chapter on meta-leadership in the McGraw-Hill *Homeland Security Handbook* (2012).

McNulty is the principal author of the NPLI's case studies on leadership decision making in the Boston Marathon bombing response, innovation in the response to Hurricane Sandy, and the professional and political interface in the Deepwater Horizon response, drawing upon his firsthand research as well as extensive interviews with leaders involved in the responses.

McNulty co-founded Harvard Business Publishing's conference business and served as its director for six years. He produced thought leadership events around the world working with some of the most celebrated executives and management experts. He also developed custom programs in collaboration with leading companies such as Accenture, Coca-Cola, SAS, UPS, Visa, and others. He is a frequent speaker and moderator at business events.

McNulty holds a bachelor's degree in economics (with honors) from the University of Massachusetts at Amherst (1981) and a master's degree in leadership from Lesley University. In this program, he explored leadership as it relates to climate change, urbanization, and other high consequence global trends.

Ame D. Wadler is managing director of health, strategy, and planning at Zeno Group. She has more than 25 years of experience in the full spectrum of public relations and public affairs for global and U.S. health care companies. With a career that spans long stints at Hill and Knowlton, Edelman Worldwide, and Burson-Marsteller, she remains committed to strategic programs that shape markets, embrace brands, and, ultimately, improve health.

Combining brand marketing and health care expertise, Wadler has played a leading role in some of the most successful brand launches in health, wellness, and beauty history, including the global launches of BOTOX Cosmetic, Claritin, Enbrel, Effexor, Lipitor, Prevage, and

Lyrica. Ame has also supported a variety of personal care products and OTC products, including Robitussin, Advil, Curel, Tums, Listerine, and Nix.

Her experience includes work in virtually every therapeutic area from allergies to headache, dermatology to ophthalmology, and everything in between. She has expertise in shaping programs to market and protect OTC and nutritional options and has worked on several planned Rx-OTC switch programs.

From litigation support to patent protection to product recalls, Wadler has a long and deep history in helping clients manage issues facing their brands.

Wadler graduated from the American University in Washington, D.C., with a bachelor of arts degree in journalism and marketing communications. She lives in Summit, New Jersey, with her husband and two sons.

About the Author

Chris Foster is the worldwide executive vice president of Burson-Marsteller. As a member of the executive leadership team, he works closely with the chairman and CEO and regional leaders on emerging strategic growth initiatives, executive-level client counsel, and business development. His expertise includes public health, life sciences, financial services, energy, and travel/tourism. He has worked across global public relations agencies, management consulting firms, trade associations, and national political campaigns.

Foster has led national and global public awareness and communications campaigns for organizations such as the U.S. Department of Defense, Centers for Medicare and Medicaid Services, Social Security Administration, Pfizer, AstraZeneca, Amgen, and Intel. He specializes in working with the federal government and private companies on understanding reputation risk and leveraging communications analytics to drive enterprise-wide strategy.

Foster is on the board of directors of a variety of organizations, including the International Association for Measurement of Communications (vice chair); Inroads, Inc.; and Burgundy Farms Country

Day School. He is also a current member of the executive leadership council. Named to the 2008 PRWeek "40 Under 40" list, Foster has been a guest lecturer at Columbia University School of Continuing Studies—Communications Department; University of Maryland, School of Journalism; and Western Kentucky University.

Foster wrote the "Reputation Analytics & Corporate Strategy" chapter published within the NYSE Corporate Governance Guide in November 2014.

He earned an MS in applied behavioral counseling from the Johns Hopkins University and a BA in philosophy from the University of Virginia.

Index

Business process and
   infrastructure, 96
"Buy-in," 94–95
Byrne, Erin, 25–30

Capability assessment, 31
Cardiovascular disease
   medications company, 8–9
CEB (Corporate Executive
   Board), 65–66
Change, constant, 4–5
Change management, 94–96
Change road map, 95
Chef (movie), 13
"Closed-loop" culture, 111
Co-creation, 4, 66–67
Co-evolution, 67–68
Cognitive computing, 30
Collaboration, 4
Communication:
   in change management, 96
   current expectations in, 45
   digital, 26–30, 73–79
   traditional, 5–6, 26–30, 73–79
   in traditional organizations, 3
Competitive factor, reputation as,
   56–57
Computing, cognitive, 30
Confirmation bias, 103
Content creation, 4, 114
Controlled trials, randomized, 93
Conversations, tracking, 10–12
Corporate Executive Board
   (CEB), 65–66
COSHAR Foundation, 9
Credit histories, customer, 92
Crisis, psychology of, 104–108

Crisis leadership, 99–110
Crisis management:
   crisis leadership versus, 103–104
   Reputation Strategy versus,
      38–39
   traditional, 74, 76
Crisis response planning, 100–101
Crowdsourcing, 4
Crowther, Yasmin, 60–61
Culture:
   "closed-loop," 111
   data-driven, 1–3
   reputation, 89–97
Curiosity, 103
Customer credit histories, 92
Customer engagement, 65
Customer experience, 64, 69, 70,
   90–91
Customer loyalty, 64–66, 90
Customer profiling, 9–10

Dark matter of marketing, 33–34
Data:
   distribution, decentralizing, 111
   relevance, assessing, 14
Data analytics, 60
Data-driven cultures, 1–3
Data science. *See also specific topics*
   about, 18
   behavioral economics and, 21
   business intelligence versus, 20
   centralizing, 111
   judgment and, 19
Davis, Marty, 18
Decentralization, 85, 111
Decisions, delegating to software
   applications, 2

Wadler, Ame, 43–45, 46–47,
   48–50
Warner-Lambert, 47
Watson project, 30

Word of mouth, 28, 76–77
Words That Work (Luntz), 114

Xiaomi, 67